All About

Sir Walter Raleigh

All About
Sir Walter Raleigh

Henrietta Buckmaster

with illustrations by
H. B. Vestal

W. H. ALLEN
LONDON
1965

© Henrietta Buckmaster, 1964
First British edition, 1965
Photoset by Cox & Sharland Ltd.,
Southampton,
Printed in Great Britain by
Fletcher & Son, Ltd.,
Norwich,
for the publishers,
W. H. Allen & Company,
Essex Street, London W.C.2.
Bound by,
Richard Clay & Co. Ltd.,
Bungay, Suffolk.

Contents

For Michael Jaffe
with my love

1
Ambitious Youth

The gales that sprang up around the Azores tore at the English ships, split the seams, toppled the mainmasts, and swept overboard any man foolish enough to keep the watch. Yet to stay in the holds of the stinking ships on that summer day of 1578 was to die of seasickness.

Sir Humphrey Gilbert, commanding the little fleet, was a master mariner though he hated the sea. He hated it for being without mercy and for destroying a man's ambitions. This gale had sent even more of his hopes to the bottom of the sea. He might struggle on deck and tug at ropes with his own hands to give his men courage, but he knew that in the end these were empty gestures. His battered ships would never succeed in reaching new lands to claim for Queen Elizabeth.

Gilbert's young half brother, Walter Raleigh, also disliked the sea. Disliked? He *loathed* it, but he already knew that the sea, under his queen, was the inescapable road to fame and fortune. Young Raleigh fought the wind for the ropes. He lashed and battened down sails, as desperate as any common seaman. But all the time he was obliged to face the fact that the Spaniards had won.

True, the English ships had ventured into Spanish

waters. True also that this was asking for trouble. But Spain always stood in the way of England's and Englishmen's ambitions. It almost seemed that these gales had come at the bidding of the Spaniards, who now lurked in their ships just out of sight in coves and inlets. From their positions of safety the Spaniards were watching the gales do their work for them.

When the calm finally came, Humphrey Gilbert and Raleigh succeeded in slipping away with their battered ships and creeping into a safe harbour for repairs.

Walter Raleigh was approximately twenty-four years old at this time (both 1552 and 1554 are given as his year of birth). And he was wild with ambition. In those days ambition could be fulfilled only by powerful family connections or by daring. Because he was the younger son of a poor Devon gentleman, he was forced to rely on daring.

Younger sons had a hard time. If they were born without quick wits, then they had better have good looks. If they were born without much sense, then they had better be blessed with abundant charm. Walter was born with quick wits, good looks, a keen mind, and a great deal of charm.

Of course there was also his family heritage of adventure to quicken his nerve. Living in Devon, close to the English Channel, Walter had known from babyhood the men who manned the ships and sailed the seas. Rough, hard-voiced, daring, they had looked on strange lands and great seas; and they had wild and wonderful tales to tell. His own half brothers — Humphrey and John Gilbert — had been knighted as "the finest seamen" of their day. Sir Francis Drake, the great navigator, was his cousin; and the famous sailor, Sir Richard Grenville, was another cousin. In fact, Raleigh once said that in time of trouble he could summon with a call a hundred of his kinsmen.

Most of these Devonshire seamen made their living by bold methods. Many of them were privateers, which was a polite name for pirates. England, like many other nations in the sixteenth century, commissioned privately owned ships to assist her weak navy in time of war. These ships, or privateers, attacked merchant ships of enemy nations and sank or robbed them.

In 1578 Spain virtually controlled the great seaways. She had established herself in both North and South America, as well as in the West Indies and along the coast of Africa. Her great ships, four stories high, brought the wealth of conquered kings to Spain. Englishmen like Drake, Martin Frobisher, and John Hawkins were challenging this power by waylaying and boarding the lofty ships. Through the English Channel and past the Devon coast, they triumphantly carried the gold, jewels, and spices which they had snatched from the Spanish holds.

During the first Queen Elizabeth's reign, Englishmen believed that the whole world lay stretched out before England. But everywhere the English seamen turned, Spain blocked the way with her massive fleets.

When he was about seventeen, young Raleigh had left Oxford University. He needed powerful patrons to launch him on a career, but his adventuring relatives were off on the seven seas. All he had were roistering young friends who needed as much help as he did. Little is known about him during these years. He probably fought in France. He may have been in Flanders. Often he was in trouble.

By the time Raleigh was in his mid-twenties, his half brother Sir Humphrey Gilbert was looking around for a man he could trust. Walter was too striking an individual to be ignored. He had a fierce temper and a staggering pride. More than six feet tall — at a time when Englishmen tended to shortness — he was also extremely handsome, with black curly hair and dark eyes. To his friends he gave candour, affection, and loyalty — comparatively rare virtues in an age when few men trusted each other. There were those, however, who complained bitterly that he used his height to look down upon men.

Sir Humphrey Gilbert had already lived his share of adventure and had been much honoured by the Queen. Now he eyed and appraised his young relative. Gilbert wanted new worlds to conquer, and so did Raleigh. Every way a man looked he could see the unknown and its challenges. Humphrey Gilbert understood that men like himself were making England into a great nation, and young Raleigh was blood of his blood.

Like many others, Gilbert was obsessed by the dream of finding a northwest passage to Asia. He went to the Queen with his plan. She listened and nodded, her bright eyes shrewd and her long slender fingers tapping. Then she asked the familiar questions: How would he pay for this proposed voyage of exploration? How would it profit the Queen of England?

Gilbert had a scheme. It included taking Newfoundland and the West Indies for the Queen. But he was foolish enough to tell Elizabeth about it. She stamped her foot angrily. Newfoundland was fair prey—it belonged to no one. But the West Indies belonged to Spain, and her whole state policy was built on peace. She was very angry. If he had *acted* and told her later, *that* would have been a different matter.

Gilbert was not a courtier. He did not understand such subtle language. But Walter Raleigh listened and learned. The Queen, for all her anger, did not wish to spoil any chance to increase England's wealth and power. The Privy Council, a group of important men who advised the Queen, gave the brothers a patent to find and claim "any remote and barbarous lands" provided they were "not already possessed by Christians."

The two half brothers quickly raised the money for the ships and men, and set sail toward the Azores, a group of islands in the North Atlantic. Spanish spies, who were everywhere, watched the sailing. Orders were given to intercept the small English fleet at all costs. But those southwesterly gales of June 1578 did the work for the Spanish. When Gilbert and Raleigh crept into a safe harbour with their battered ships, the Spaniards knew that it would be weeks before they could sail again.

Meanwhile the Spaniards watched and waited. After the repairs had finally been made, it was almost winter. Only fools would set out into the teeth of winter storms, but Englishmen were fools. Sir Humphrey tried again. Near Cape Verde, Spanish ships swooped down on the small fleet. The battle was swift and terrible. One English ship went down with all hands; Raleigh himself was wounded. Gilbert took what was left and struggled home.

But Walter could not take his eyes from the western sea. His wounds mended, and with his lone ship he started off across that hazardous grey, lashing Atlantic, searching for a prize and battling with the lonely ocean. At length the storms made a wall he could not pass through. His provisions had reached the starvation point, and his men threatened to mutiny. With weary reluctance, he turned back.

Raleigh and Gilbert had lost all their investment in this ill-fated sea venture. Worse, they had lost the Queen's investment as well, and she never took such losses with grace. Both Gilbert and Raleigh were required to pay fines to the government.

Walter was almost wild with frustrated ambition. In such a state, where could he go?

There was always Ireland!

Ireland had never really been conquered, though the English had been there for generations. Irish chiefs had sworn a kind of loyalty to England until Elizabeth's father, Henry VIII, broke with the Pope in Rome and established the Church of England. This brought open conflict with the Catholic Church, and the Catholic Irish badgered the English with constant uprisings. The English regarded the Irish as creatures of Spain and the Pope, and put down the risings with bloody ferocity.

An English gentleman who made a name for himself fighting against the Irish drew the best kind of attention at home. Humphrey Gilbert, for instance, had won his knighthood in Ireland. So in 1580 Raleigh crossed the Irish Sea to seek his own belated fortune as captain of an infantry company.

Ireland brought out a side of Raleigh that was savage and violent, qualities seldom associated with him. His familiar enemy, the Spanish, were supporting the Irish with guns and money. He spent the year in bloody fighting, putting down Irish rebellions, quarrelling with his superiors, and dreaming of home.

Several gallant acts of his added lustre to the Raleigh name. He took a stronghold of three hundred men by a ruse and held it with eleven men until reinforcements arrived. He rescued a wounded friend from the very hands of the enemy, then single-handed held a ford against a small army, "standing with a pistol in one hand and a quarterstaff in the other" until his men got across.

But oddly enough it was his quarrels with his superiors which brought him to the attention of the Queen. He claimed that the Lord Deputy and the Commanding General were turning Ireland into "a lost land — not a commonwealth but a common woe." In December of 1581 he won his release from service and returned to England.

Some of Raleigh's opinions reached the Queen. She knew these Raleighs and Gilberts. They were no fools. Raleigh was called before the Privy Council to confront the Lord Deputy of Ireland himself.

Elizabeth was there and, according to a contemporary, Raleigh "got the Queen's ear in a trice, and she began to be taken with his elocution and loved to hear his reasons to her demands." His low voice must have been pleasing to her who had so many shrill, clamorous moments in her life.

The fact that he was very handsome was no disadvantage either. The Queen liked the men and women around her to be quick, witty, handsome, and intelligent. She was a remarkable woman — shrewd, able, unsentimental where England was concerned — although in her private life she was lonely and capricious. She knew that

nearly everyone wished to take advantage of her for his own gain. But if a man brought her a daring and imaginative plan that would widen the horizons of her beloved country and bring money to its empty coffers, she liked that man and helped him to his fortune.

She liked Raleigh, though she mixed her liking with her usual caution. She talked with him often, and continued to enjoy his replies. Her powerful treasurer, William Cecil (Lord Burghley), and her equally powerful secretary of state, Sir Francis Walsingham, continued to probe him for comments on Ireland.

Raleigh was also sent on a delicate mission to Holland, which was then struggling to be free of Spain. But none of this activity was important enough to satisfy him. Raleigh felt he was only marking time, for the Queen showed no special favour beyond her command that he remain at Court. He chafed, and sought passionately for reasons, and wrote poetry.

There is a story that one day when Raleigh stood with the Queen in a palace room, he scratched the following words on a windowpane with the diamond on his dagger hilt:

Fain would I rise, yet fear I to fall.

After a moment the Queen took the dagger and scratched this sentence beneath:

If thy heart fail thee, rise not at all.

Whether or not the story is true, Raleigh henceforth seemed to act upon some such advice. No one could ever call him faint-hearted.

His rise was swift.

2
The Man of Action

The Queen called Raleigh her "Oracle." She admired his wit and his bold advice, and loved his grace, his manner, and his looks, which were not a courtier's. Her eyes were on him more and more.

She also showed her approval in more practical ways. She gave him lands and estates in England and Ireland, and the lease on the greater part of a palace along the River Thames. In this palace, called Durham House, he entertained like a prince. In addition, the Queen gave him the monopoly on wine licenses, which brought him a large revenue—as well as much jealousy. And the next year he received a highly profitable license to export woollen broadcloth.

About this time—probably in 1585—the Queen knighted Raleigh; now he was Sir Walter. She made him Lieutenant of Cornwall and Vice-Admiral for both Devon and Cornwall, and appointed him Lord Warden of the Stannaries. This last position brought under his control all the tin mining of Cornwall.

Within a year Raleigh was spoken of as one of the most powerful men in England. An elected member of Parliament, he dreamed of sitting among the Queen's advisors on the Privy Council. In 1587 Elizabeth made him Captain of the Queen's Guard, an exceedingly important post. He was responsible for the Queen's safety and, when on duty, stood by the door of her apartment.

But while the Queen wished Raleigh near her, she did not wish him to have *too* much power. Perhaps she understood that he relied too much on externals — his charm, his looks, his wit. She may have realised that he needed study and discipline to be the kind of statesman she had always chosen so unerringly. His very quickness and wit — his contempt for bores — were a kind of liability. On the other hand, her own caprice and contrariness may have kept him from realising a great destiny.

During the years of his meteoric rise, restlessness rode like an ape on his back. When he begged permission to undertake a colonising expedition to that "new England towards the sunset," she agreed to finance it. With high excitement he set the builders to work on a ship of unusual design. He plunged into plans that would make the expedition a fresh and vigorous assault on the unknown. At last, when all was ready and the crews were assembled, the Queen sent him word — he must not go.

He could hardly believe it. The expedition would go but not Raleigh. Raleigh must stay safe at home. To his brother Humphrey Gilbert, who was in joint command, he sent the Queen's decision, adding, "I have sent you a token from Her Majesty, an anchor guided by a lady." It was his gallant effort to be ironic at the fate reserved for him.

His ship, the *Bark-Raleigh,* went in his name, but she was doomed to play as disappointing a role in the expedition as her owner. After two days at sea, tossed by a fierce storm, her crew forced the captain to turn home.

Gilbert continued across the Atlantic with the three ships remaining. He reached Newfoundland in a heavy fog and claimed this grim, unpromising land in the Queen's name. Then he explored carefully down the coast, claiming what he could for England. In the dense fog, one of the ships ran onto a sand bar. More than one hundred men perished aboard the wrecked vessel.

Because his men were restless, Gilbert pretended to be untroubled and sat on deck in the midst of the storms. One night the waves were "high as the Pyramids" and tossed the two remaining ships like bits of broken wood. Experienced old seamen had never seen such a storm before, and soon they lost almost all control of the ships. During the worst of the gale, the crew were amazed — and heartened — to see Humphrey sitting on the deck with a book in his hand. He called out cheerfully above the wind, "We are as near to heaven by sea as by land!"

By midnight, however, the lights on his halyard had disappeared. The mountainous waves had claimed him and his men. Queen Elizabeth took this disaster as a proof that she had saved Raleigh's life. As for Raleigh, he grieved for his half brother. He had admired and loved Gilbert all his life.

The failure of the voyage only sharpened Raleigh's eagerness to command his own expedition to success. He planned, he plotted, he dreamed of ways to get around the Queen. It was not only personal ambition which drove him, but an obsessive belief that, until the Spanish power was broken, England would remain a weak nation. Colonisation was the answer to the power of Spain. Let England settle Englishmen along the coasts of America, and see what the Spaniards would do then!

He persuaded a few Englishmen to invest their money and hope in his dream of English colonies. He himself spent a fortune on ships and supplies for a new expedition. In 1584 two of his ships reached what is now North Carolina. But again Raleigh had been forced to remain in England with the Queen. His men, however, established friendly contact with the Indians and brought back, as guests of England, two Indian chiefs. They also brought back furs, skins, and glowing accounts of the land they had seen.

The next year, the Queen gave Raleigh a patent to colonise the land above the Spanish territories of Florida. She agreed that all land taken in the name of England should be named *Virginia,* in honour of her, the Virgin Queen. This was a vast unmapped, undefined land, but a favourite saying of the time was, "There is no sea unnavigable nor land uninhabitable."

Raleigh had better hopes of actually sailing in command of this expedition, for he could not believe that Elizabeth's wilfulness would repeat itself a third time. He spent the months of preparation poring over every document that related to the North American coast. He talked with every seaman who knew the coastal waters, and carefully selected the men who would compose the crew. In addition, he recruited specialists for his staff. Among them were John White, an expert cartographer and the first artist to use water colours, and Thomas Hariot, a geographer and mathematician. Then there was Thomas Cavendish, the second Englishman to circumnavigate the globe. These were men who would be a credit to any commander of an expedition.

Raleigh worked doggedly to raise enough money to equip his ships, and he chose settlers who had stamina and were willing to hazard the unknown risks of "Virginia."

At the last moment, however, he was told to remain behind with the Queen. Once again she refused to allow him to leave her court.

Raleigh watched the fleet sail in April of 1585 with his cousin, Sir Richard Grenville, in command. Grenville was perhaps the only man whom Raleigh would have trusted to do and see things as he would himself.

In October, Grenville brought back reports of both success and failure.

Success lay in the tangible wealth borne in the holds of his ships ... more than £500,000 worth of gold, silver, pearls, ivory, sugar, and spices captured from a Spanish ship near the Bermudas. Failure lay in the attempted

colonisation, which died before it was born.

Grenville had landed the settlers at Roanoke as he had planned, promising to bring them supplies before Easter. He then sailed for England, by way of the West Indies. Word had reached him of a Spanish treasure ship near the Bermudas, and he shared Raleigh's conviction that to prey on Spanish ships was an Englishman's duty.

Almost immediately the abandoned Roanoke settlers found themselves in serious difficulties. The season was too late for them to clear the land and plant crops, and the Indians became threatening. Grenville did not return with their supplies, but in June Sir Francis Drake appeared fresh from the burning of St. Augustine and profitable raids in the West Indies. The settlers greeted him in some panic and begged to be taken home. Drake agreed.

When Grenville finally sailed into Roanoke with a relief ship, he was mystified by the colony's complete disappearance. He left fifteen volunteers, and supplies for two years. But this was an insufficient number of men to cope with the problems of a wilderness world.

The Queen, however, was so pleased with her share of the gold, silver, and pearls brought back by Grenville that she paid little attention to the failure of the colony. It was Raleigh who grieved over the failure and wondered, with some dread, how fifteen men could build, plant, reap, and defend themselves against Indians and winter.

He realised that a true colony must be established there as soon as possible. Such a colony would consist of families. It would be made up of men and women who were carefully supplied for all emergencies and whose future depended on their successful adjustment to a wilderness world.

Raleigh talked urgently with the brilliant men who had been with Grenville. He probed and questioned. What did White, the cartographer, mean by *these* lines on the map? What did Hariot, the geographer, feel about the land and its possibilities?

Hariot had been much impressed by the tobacco and

potato fields of the Indians. Raleigh asked for every detail.

During the next months he laid even more careful plans. By 1587 he had recruited over a hundred colonists — men and women who were willing and anxious to build homes and remain in the New World, to make a life and rear families. Each man was to receive five hundred acres, and grants of additional acres would be determined by his investment in the company.

The group set out in three ships, with supplies.

One ship was obliged, by storms and leaking seams, to turn back temporarily. The others went on. There was no easy assurance, no previous example to guide them. Nothing quite like this had been tried before.

Their courage failed somewhat when they reached Roanoke and discovered that the fifteen men left by Grenville had been killed by the Indians. But when the third vessel finally arrived with its supplies, their spirits rose.

No one had expected a life without dangers. The colonists built and planted. And when the first baby was born, the whole community named her "Virginia." Virginia Dare, the first English child to be born in America, gave substance to a dream.

But not quite enough substance. The Indians could not be won over, and the soil remained stubborn and unyielding. The colonists were shaken with doubts and persuaded their governor to return to England with urgent pleas to Raleigh to remember them with reinforcements and provisions.

Raleigh received the message with great concern, for many things had changed at home. His heart was in the Virginia venture, but the climate at home had grown stormy with fears of a Spanish invasion.

He was determined, however, to keep his promise to the colonists. Under the greatest difficulties he secured the use of two ships, which he promptly dispatched with the necessary provisions. But the sailors could not resist the lure of piracy. Near the Azores they began to attack and board Spanish merchant ships. Before long they, too, were boarded. Set on by French pirates, the English ships were stripped of all their provisions.

Limping back into harbour, they sealed the fate of the colonists. Help was now out of the question — and for a reason that was overwhelming: the Spanish Armada.

A powerful fleet was sailing like doom toward England.

Philip II, King of Spain, had decided that the time had come to challenge English rule at home and abroad. Thirty years before, he had been husband to Elizabeth's half sister, Mary Tudor, then Queen of England. Although Mary had been dead for many years, Philip had never relinquished his claim to the English crown.

Through most of the year 1587, English spies had brought word from every capital of Europe of some momentous plans in Spain for invading England. The air was filled with rumours and disputed facts. Drake slipped into the Spanish harbour of Cadiz and destroyed the provisions which Philip had been gathering for a year. But no one — and least of all the Queen — could quite bring himself to acknowledge the stupendous nature of Philip's plans.

But all through the spring of 1588, the Queen's dock-yards echoed to saws and hammers and the shouts of men labouring night and day. Rumours spread faster than truth. The Queen, meanwhile, swayed back and forth between peace and war.

Raleigh, Hawkins, and Hariot drew up plans for ships of deeper keel and lower decks and swifter sailing power. Drake chafed at restraints and begged to be allowed to meet the Spaniards halfway. But the Queen still cried, "No war, gentlemen, no war!"

Late in May, 1588, Philip's vast fleet started for England. One hundred and thirty mighty ships of war, with twenty-seven thousand men aboard, raised their sails and set their compasses.

England was only just beginning to test her sea power. Elizabeth's entire navy consisted of thirty-five ships, but many of these ships were based on a new concept of manoeuverability.

Although Raleigh's skill at sea was known to everyone, he had been given no ship to command. When he rushed back from his estates in Ireland, the Queen sent him promptly to the West Country. She saw this as a chief danger spot and believed that the defence of the coasts was imperative. No one really believed that the tiny English navy could meet and match the mighty Spaniards. Instead the British coolly planned to defend every yard of English soil, step by step.

Raleigh rode up and down the countryside calling on the men of Devon, who had always come at his summons. The defences he built were as good as any man could make them—provided he took no sleep and whipped others to match his pace!

In addition, Raleigh and Lord Charles Howard of Effingham, the Lord Admiral, had to fight the Queen's counsellors in London, who wished to disperse her small navy to various danger spots. To Raleigh and Howard a concentration of power at Plymouth was imperative to deal the crucial blow. They worked with remarkable unity, and somehow prevailed.

The days of waiting during that July made their nerves tight as a drum. Somewhere along the French coast was an enemy fleet of such formidable strength that the whole future of England could be shaped by it.

On the night of July 19, by the light of a half moon, a vast rolling crescent of ships appeared to lookouts on the English cliffs like an apparition, silently, dreadfully filling the sea. The sight was more formidable than their wildest fears; the ships stretched back to the horizon.

The lookout flashed the news. The little English ships eased themselves onto the moonlit waters and, without warning, opened fire with their new long-range guns.

The magnificent, unwieldy floating fortresses of the Spanish Armada showed their astonishment. They too had long-range guns, but where could they aim them? The small ships darted and probed, not waiting for the slow stately aim of the Spanish guns.

By dawn, the Spaniards were filled with dismay. Like magnificent horses worried by small dogs, their great warships could not defend themselves. Their admiral, the Duke of Medina Sidonia, increased the sail, but the ships' speed of two miles an hour was unchanged. His only chance was to join his force with that of the Duke of Parma, who would come forth from Holland to the rendezvous.

But Drake sent fire-ships filled with explosives among the Spanish vessels. In their terror the Spanish cut their cables. Ships were flung together. Some ran before the wind; others turned and tried to meet these English madmen.

For nine days this sea fight ranged up and down the Channel. Raleigh described it as "that morrice [Morris] dance upon the waters," wherein the mightiest fleet in the modern world was "by thirty of Her Majesty's own ships of war, and a few of our own merchants . . . beaten and shuffled together, from the Lizard in Cornwall, first to Portland—from Portland to Calais—and from Calais driven with squibs from their anchors, were chased . . . round about Scotland and Ireland where . . . a great part of them were crushed against the rocks, and those that landed were broken, slain, or taken, coupled in halters to be shipped into England. . . . They did not . . . so much as sink or take one ship . . . or even burn as much as one sheep-cote of this land."

It was an incredible victory—a victory that not only established England as a great power but marked the end of Spanish power.

The Armada had sailed four thousand miles in five months. Of the one hundred and thirty ships that had set sail, only sixty-five returned.

3

Defeats and Disappointments

Just at this point, another man began to rise in the Queen's favour. He was the Earl of Essex. Twenty-two years old and a distant relative of the Queen, he was as handsome and tall as Raleigh, with blond hair instead of black. He was also headstrong, spoiled, determined, dangerous.

To Raleigh, who had waited patiently for many years to win the Queen's favour, the sudden rise of Essex was almost too bitter to bear. He knew that this impetuous young man would be no stable counsellor for a queen who was old enough to be his mother. Raleigh, on the other hand, understood many of her needs as a lonely sovereign.

Raleigh was a man in his fullest maturity, handsomer than most, wiser than most. He was a poet, a scholar, and a philosopher — curious and qualified to explore the mysteries of science but also accustomed to speaking his mind without fear or favour.

He sincerely tried to avoid a rupture with Essex, but Essex saw Raleigh as always standing in his way. One hot July evening Raleigh stood outside the Queen's apartment in his silver armour, which he wore in his

powerful position as her Captain of the Guard. Essex was within, speaking to the Queen. He raised his voice, so that Raleigh could hear, and said accusingly that the Queen's desire was "only to please that knave, Raleigh, for whose sake she would both grieve me and my love."

The Queen answered sharply that he had no reason to disdain Raleigh. But Essex was determined to behave like a spoiled and headstrong boy, and repeated his insulting charges. The Queen refused to answer his angry words, and at length turned away. Whereupon Essex rushed from her presence, threatening to go and "die in the wars in Holland."

Elizabeth sent after him, though her messengers did not reach Essex until he had boarded a ship for Holland. They brought him back like a runaway child. Essex challenged Raleigh to a duel, but the Queen forbade any fighting. Essex, however, had achieved what he wanted: the Queen's attention. Against her better judgment she was flattered. Honours, one by one, began to come to him. Soon no one was as important to Elizabeth as Essex.

Raleigh tried to move swiftly, confident that the greatest gift he could give the Queen was a vast new settlement in America. He knew her personal greed as well as her ambitions for England. The Spanish danger had been cleared away. Now was the time to strike boldly for his vision of a new world — and his own personal ambitions.

Twice Elizabeth promised support for an American journey; twice she withdrew it. All other moves he made were somehow countered by Essex. At length Raleigh was forced into a manoeuver that might have spelled the end for him. He withdrew to his estates in Ireland. It was a gamble, but absence *has* been known to make the heart grow fonder.

"My Lord of Essex hath chased Mr. Raleigh from Court," wrote one gossip to another, "and hath confined him to Ireland."

This was the explanation which Essex' friends hoped to have accepted. To have Raleigh as an enemy would add a certain lustre to Essex' reputation. What Essex had not foreseen was the danger from Raleigh's old supporter, Lord Burghley.

Burghley had been the Queen's chief minister as long

as most Englishmen could remember. She trusted his wisdom, and knew that his devotion was unswerving. He was now a sick old man, but he had spent a lifetime in her service and had never failed her.

Burghley warned her of Essex. He warned her carefully and discreetly and, in spite of her infatuation, she heeded his wisdom. She heeded not only the wise old man but also his son, Robert Cecil. Young Cecil was a remarkable figure. At thirty he seemed to have all his father's powers of statecraft, though in physical appearance he was small and weak.

The Queen must have been as aware as Lord Burghley that Robert was the only man to take her old minister's place. Step by step he was mounting behind his father, and presently he would be in the councils of the Queen.

It was a strange situation. A sick old man and his puny son were setting themselves calmly against a glittering and peerless young noble who was adored by a queen. But since Elizabeth was first a queen and second a woman, she refused Essex the power he wanted. He wished to be her prime adviser. He wished to influence English history.

Meanwhile Raleigh, in Ireland, used his time to improve his Irish estates and to write poetry. But in December of 1589 he returned to England. Perhaps he had word from his friends to return, or perhaps he sensed that something in the air was auspicious for him.

Raleigh's enemies were very irritated to see that the Queen greeted him as though truly glad to have him back. Essex had been a sore trial, rude, demanding. Although he was still Elizabeth's golden youth, Raleigh was her Wit, her Oracle. Try him though she did, he was always faithful.

In the strange rivalry between Essex and Raleigh, it seemed that any rise in favour on the part of one man foretold the fall from favour of the other.

Within a few weeks of Raleigh's return, Essex took

a wife in a secret marriage. Nothing he could have done would have offended the Queen more deeply. She was half demented on the subject of marriage — and of secret marriages in particular. She took the marriages of her favourites as a personal affront, and their position with the Queen was thereby forfeited. She refused to see the offenders. She harried them in every way she could short of ruin, and she usually committed either husband or wife to prison.

Historians have puzzled over Elizabeth's own refusal to marry and her hysteria when her courtiers did. Perhaps the reason lay in her wretched·childhood. She had suffered terribly from the caprices of her father, Henry VIII, who had ordered her mother, Anne Boleyn, beheaded. As queen, Elizabeth used her unmarried state in one clever diplomatic move after the other. For years she offered herself as a possible bride to this European prince and that one, always withdrawing when she had accomplished her objective — a treaty or a concession.

In her heart she must have known that as queen she could never give up her independence to a husband.

In her anger and hurt at Essex over his secret marriage, she turned to Raleigh, long loved and long loving. *He* would not fail her. She made him Vice-Admiral of the Fleet under Lord Thomas Howard. She gave him additional lands and honours. Most wonderful of all, the Queen appointed him to full command of a fleet of English ships which would attack the Isthmus of Panama and the Spanish treasure fleets.

Raleigh was at a peak of power. His hopes were close to realisation. He had not a doubt in the world that the expedition would bring home glory and riches. Exhilarated and happy, he worked day and night to make sure that he had the best seamen, ample supplies, and the sturdiest of ships. The only flaw was the contrary winds in the Thames. They delayed the sailing for several days.

The delay was fatal. It gave the Queen a chance to

perform her old cruel trick. Raleigh was not to be allowed to sail after all. His command would be taken over by Sir Martin Frobisher, famous as a seaman but hated by sailors.

Raleigh was in despair, but what could he do? He extracted the promise that he might go as far as the coast of Spain with his fleet.

With the wind in his sails, he was tempted to risk the Queen's anger and sail on as he desired, but before he reached Cape Finisterre he learned from a captive Spaniard that King Philip had ordered the Spanish treasure ships to delay their ocean crossing.

This was dismaying news. It altered the whole purpose of the expedition. Raleigh and his commanders found a quiet anchorage and held a council.

They decided to divide into two squadrons. One, under Sir John Burroughs, was to sail to the Azores and intercept any ships from the East or West Indies. The other squadron, under Frobisher, would make its inconspicuous way along the coast of Spain to draw attention away from Burroughs.

Raleigh sailed for home.

He went with apprehension. He had every reason to believe that he would be arrested — not because he had delayed in obeying the Queen's command, but because he knew that the Queen had discovered his secret.

Raleigh also had taken a wife.

4

Bess Throckmorton

Raleigh was now a man of forty. He knew very well how terrible was the Queen's anger against any marriage. Through all the seesaw of his fortunes, his frustrations, and his feud with Essex, he had remained the Queen's Oracle, her "Water." These affectionate names showed her deep regard.

But he must have longed for some stability and peace in the terrible uncertainty of his life, with its jealousies and trickeries. His scientific experiments, his intelligent and creative interest in scientists, his writing of poetry, his brilliant intellect and strong practical vision of new worlds, were all wonderfully satisfying but impersonal.

Raleigh was part way to the Azores when the word spread through the Court that he had secretly married. *Secretly married.* Probably no other two words could have angered the Queen so much. They meant his downfall.

In stark amazement his enemies asked how a man who had struggled so hard to fulfill his ambitions could suddenly throw his future away in a gesture. And to think he had done it for Elizabeth Throckmorton! How could she — she of all the ladies of the court — win this man who had avoided marriage for so many years?

Elizabeth Throckmorton was looked at afresh. She came from a good family (her father had been a Member of Parliament and an ambassador to France). A Maid of Honour to the Queen, she was intelligent and witty, tall, graceful, blue-eyed and yellow-haired, but she was in her late twenties. This was old for a woman in those days. Moreover, she had no special fortune nor connections which would have made it worth the risk that Raleigh took. Could he have married her for love?

He had indeed. As time would prove it was a deep, tender love that not only survived but fed upon all the high drama of their life together.

The secrecy with which Raleigh had been able to do his wooing intrigued the Court and wounded the Queen. He, as Captain of the Guard, and Bess Throckmorton, as Maid of Honour, were in the same room day after day, but always under the jealous eyes of the Queen. Even to exchange messages must have been difficult.

The Queen's anger was fed by her imagination. These two who had stood so close and affectionately to her must all the time have been fooling her. No doubt they had bribed pages and tipped gardeners to be alone. Watermen had probably rowed them many a dark evening up the Thames in order to escape her watchfulness.

The Queen refused to see Bess Throckmorton, but Bess showed a courage that had much valiance in it, for she had to bear all her fears alone. Finally, after several days, she was sent to the Tower.

Her husband's enemies waited eagerly as each day bore his ship closer to England. His friends waited with sinking hearts, not daring to show too much kindness to Bess, though secretly they were doing all in their power for her.

The blow did not fall immediately upon his return to England. In fact, for some reason, the Queen waited nearly six weeks before ordering his arrest and imprisonment in the Tower.

The Tower was a grim, four-turreted building by the Thames. Part of its walls survived, according to legend, from the days of Julius Caesar. William the Conqueror and all subsequent Kings had used it as both palace and prison, torture house and place of execution. The Queen's own mother had been beheaded within the Tower. Even the Queen herself had once been held prisoner there before she assumed the throne. Scarcely a famous man or woman had not been within its fearsome walls at one time or another.

Raleigh's wife was held in a separate cell, and no pleas were strong enough to allow him even a word with the imprisoned Bess.

Raleigh drew on his knowledge of the Queen and his affection for her. He wrote her ardent letters, protesting his lifetime devotion. He implored Robert Cecil, his own good friend, to intercede. He begged everyone with a little power to put in a word for the Raleighs.

If he regretted what he had done, he gave no sign. In this he was unlike Essex, who had sent his bride away and insisted he did not really care for her, until the Queen's rage had passed.

Raleigh and Bess hoped that their punishment would be brief. Essex had been forgiven within a few months, though his wife was not allowed at Court. The Raleighs had a hope that the same course might be followed with them.

But against Raleigh, the Queen's anger was more intemperate than against any of her other favourites. Perhaps she was angry because of his position and his age. Unlike Essex, he had no powerful title. Everything he had he owed to the Queen. His smallest ambition was dependent on her favour. He could not move in any direction without her support. Probably he, of all her favourites, had seemed the one most bound to her, the one least likely to desert her for a wife. At forty, why should he want a wife?

Although Raleigh and Bess could not see each other, their quarters were comfortable. He was allowed to transact business, and none of his estates was taken from him. Above all, he was not deprived of his powerful position as Captain of the Guard. His own cousin, Sir George Carew, was made his keeper. Raleigh tried to see hopeful signs in all of this.

His helplessness, however, was very hard to bear. He was aware that once again his fall from favour coincided with Essex' rise. And Essex was placing as many friends as possible in positions around the Queen

Raleigh's helplessness continued through the weeks of early summer. Then suddenly and ironically his release came — came because he was indispensable. His fleet, the fleet he had led as far as the Azores, had gone on to seize the greatest prize ever brought home in Elizabeth's reign.

Sir John Burroughs, in the ship which Raleigh had built for himself, had captured a great Portuguese carrack from the East Indies. Built like a monstrous tower, seven decks high, and painted in dazzling colours, the *Madre de Dios* was loaded with priceless treasure. From the East came fifteen tons of ebony, five hundred tons of spices — at this time spices were almost as valuable as jewels — diamonds as big as nuts, silks, drugs, and ivory. The booty from the *Madre de Dios* as well as from other smaller ships was valued at over £500,000 (in today's valuation). This was a poetic justice for Raleigh that exceeded his dreams.

But the looting of the treasure began even before the fleet reached Dartmouth. And when the ships docked, the sailors and citizens went on an orgy of pillaging. Part of this was induced by the sailors' fury at learning that their admiral, Raleigh, had been imprisoned for taking a wife. They mutinied against their officers and broke into the Queen's share of the treasure.

Presently it seemed as though everyone in the West Country had helped himself to the booty. Since the

Queen had first claim on the treasure, her ministers were horrified. At last the Controller of the Navy, Sir John Hawkins, said aloud what everybody knew: only Raleigh could stop the wholesale stealing and re-establish order.

Robert Cecil, who had been hurriedly sent to Plymouth, wrote to his father, Lord Burghley, that Raleigh *must* be allowed his liberty even under guard.

The gates of the Tower swung open. Raleigh and one guard mounted their horses and rode at great speed to the West Country. Here he was greeted with such cries of joy and embraces that Cecil could hardly believe what he saw. Raleigh's own servants, he wrote to his father, "to the number of one hundred and forty goodly men — and also all the mariners — came to him with such shouts of joy as I never saw a man more troubled to quiet in all my life."

Raleigh knew his own worth. As Cecil watched with increasing amazement, Raleigh brought into line even the wildest of the pillagers. Having accomplished an amazing task and saved an incredible fortune for the Queen, he no longer begged. Instead he bargained. He said very clearly that the Queen's treasure would not have been endangered had he been in charge from the start. He had no intention of saving the treasure and then returning to prison.

These were bold words, for he could do nothing, really, to make them work. "My promise was not to buy my bondage but my liberty." And he reminded Lord Burghley, and through him the Queen, that his fourscore thousand pounds were "more than ever a man presented to Her Majesty as yet. If God have sent it for my ransom, I hope Her Majesty will accept it."

He had bargained shrewdly. The Queen's investment in the expedition entitled her to one-tenth of the prize: he arranged that she got half. The Londoners who had invested money received double their investment. He himself, although he had been paying interest on the money he had borrowed to finance the voyage, received

nothing but his eventual freedom and the freedom of his wife.

He emerged from prison a poor man, though he had his Bess, his freedom, and his beloved estate at Sherborne. The Queen refused to see him, so he and Bess travelled to Dorset like two young lovers on a honeymoon. There he devoted all his energies to his new roles of husband and estate manager. Although his enemies at Court were working against him, Raleigh was willing to wait.

Never were Bess and he so happy again. At Sherborne they gathered around them the friends whom Raleigh trusted and those who stirred his mind — astronomers and mathematicians, philosophers and poets. He wrote and thought and talked and planned, laying the groundwork for a dozen possible careers.

These were uncommon days for the whole world. Men's imaginations lived in a constant ferment. Ideas were rich as gold. The explorations of thought were as vivid and meaningful as the explorations by ships. Man's dominion over the forces of nature was sought by chemist and alchemist. Scientific inquirers were no longer considered magicians or dealers in devilish arts.

It had been determined that heaven was not a series of spheres moving over and around the earth, but that the earth truly lived *in* heaven. This was a moral discovery as well as a scientific one. It taught that human life was sacred. It taught a new concept of God. It lifted the old curse on man which traditional religions had imposed. It said beauty and knowledge were good, and that earth was a foretaste of heaven.

The range of the universe was now Raleigh's field of inquiry.

5

The Gilded City

The Queen appointed a deputy Captain of the Guard.
She did not strip Raleigh of the title or take away any
honours.

Raleigh went to London during the winter of 1593 to
fulfill his duties as a Member of Parliament. The Queen
still refused to see him, but she followed avidly the
debates in which he took a prominent part. He spoke
well and often, fighting vigorously for the bills he
supported, and constantly trying to rouse Parliament to
the dangers of Spain and the need to clarify England's
drifting policy.

He loved these days as a Parliamentarian. Everything
he did and said had one motive: to build England as a
great force in the world. Almost single-handed, he
fought to make his countrymen see their little fog-
enshrouded island in the North Sea as a power that
could encircle the globe.

And he saw ways of accomplishing this that were
uncommon to the time. He wanted to do it through a
series of treaties with native peoples, through justice and
fair trade and fair bargaining — not by enslavement or
terror.

So he wrote, listened, argued, pled, and used what little influence he now had. His great need, as he saw it, was to enlarge that influence, and he dreamed and planned of ways to feed the Queen's ambition. He was convinced his fortune and future lay in America. Find El Dorado . . . find the legendary city of gold.

Many men believed that there was indeed such a place. Many believed it could be found in South America. Mariners returned saying that the South American Indians claimed that a city of pure gold was hidden in the mountainous jungles above the unexplored reaches of the Orinoco River.

The Spaniards had given this legendary city its name El Dorado, meaning "The Gilded." Many believed the tale of Martinez, a Spaniard, who took an oath on his deathbed that he had been within the golden city. He said he had stood blindfolded before its emperor, whose palace was furnished with golden chairs and golden pots, and who was himself washed in turpentine and covered with gold dust every day.

Any man who had seen the dazzling riches of Peru and Mexico, the endless glories of the great Inca and Aztec empires, found no difficulty believing in El Dorado.

Raleigh studied all that had been written about these fabled lands. He talked with as many seamen as he could find who had sailed along the coasts of Guiana and around Trinidad. He was convinced that he held the clues to an unlimited wealth of gold and jewels, such as Pizarro had found among the Incas. He would conquer the land for the Queen and be its first governor.

Raleigh was persuasive. Investors looked up brightly. The Queen's government inclined an ear. Only Bess, his wife, was in despair.

They now had a son, Wat. What would he do without a father? She did all she could to hold her husband. She never doubted his love, but like most wives she wanted her husband where she could see him, not off in some far part of an unknown world, subject to dangers that defied the imagination.

But she could not hold him back. His life's dream must be accomplished. The Queen agreed to give him a patent which commissioned him to discover and conquer lands "unpossessed by any Christian prince," and also to "offend and enfeeble the king of Spain."

For Raleigh, this was the golden moment of his life. He refused to heed the mocking fear that the Queen would restrain him at the last moment. He tried to make the expedition's success so dependent on his command that it could not proceed without him.

By the first week of February, 1595, his small fleet and his officers, soldiers, and "gentlemen volunteers" were ready and waiting. One ship represented the investment of Lord Admiral Howard, a relative of Raleigh's wife. Robert Cecil and his father also put money in the expedition. These were three men who had shown Raleigh a wary friendship, and intervened with the Queen while he was out of favour.

Aboard his flagship, Raleigh had two trunks of books as well as an old friend with whom he could while away the long hours of the voyage. The friend was Lawrence Keymis, Fellow of Balliol College, Oxford, who loved Raleigh and brought his mathematical and geographic genius to the expedition.

As Raleigh waited for the tide, he tried to comfort his weeping wife and wailing child. How Bess must have longed for a Queen's messenger to prevent Raleigh's departure. But as the tide changed there was no breathless messenger arriving at the last minute to say that Her Majesty was commanding him to remain in England.

Raleigh kissed his wife and son and turned his face toward his life's ambition.

It was necessary for a sailing fleet to disperse as soon as it set sail. At the mercy of winds and waves, the ships could not stay together. Sometimes a fleet took a full week to reassemble at a prearranged rendezvous, take on water and provisions, and set out for the next port.

Raleigh had commanded that the Canary Islands be the first rendezvous. He arrived there and waited a week, but none of his other ships appeared. Finally he weighed anchor and departed for Trinidad.

Trinidad lies off the coast of what is now Venezuela, on the northern coast of South America. To Raleigh it was a new world of soft winds and warm sun and flying fishes, of stars that one did not see in England. But at Trinidad he was again disappointed to find no ships. He and his men were alone in an alien and hostile world. The Dragon's Mouth and the Serpent's Mouth were the names of the two channels that led into the island. The names did not sound inviting. Somewhere up the Dragon's Mouth was a Spanish settlement.

In his barge, Raleigh and his men explored the coast of Trinidad. He was trained to observe and evaluate what he saw: the coves and the rivers and the "very salt well-tasted" fruit that he plucked from the low-hanging mangrove trees. These could provision explorers. He observed the great pitch lake, the nature of which he did not fully understand but which he sensed could be of great importance. (A little more than three hundred years later it turned Venezuela into one of the great oil-producing countries in the world.)

He also made friends with the Indians and talked with them long into the night. They told him terrible stories of Spanish cruelty — a cruelty so ferocious that the Indians had frequently risen against the Spanish settlements on the mainland.

Raleigh found that these quiet redskinned men responded to friendliness. They were anxious to have peace. He ordered his sailors to negotiate and pay for everything they needed, and to behave in the most proper way toward the Indian women.

He showed the chiefs a picture of his own great *Cacique,* or Queen, and they fell on their knees before the miniature of Elizabeth with her white skin and red hair

and great starched ruff which they called "wings."
Whether from politeness or awe they called her a god-
dess. Raleigh assured them that with her support they
could be protected from the Spanish. He formally
annexed Trinidad in the name of the Queen, and raised
a high pole which bore the royal arms.

Raleigh knew that the Spanish settlement on Trinidad
must be destroyed in order to confirm his promises to
the Indians and protect his party when it moved to the
mainland.

With his one ship he sailed up the channel to San
Josef. Taking it by surprise, he captured the Spanish
governor, Berrio, rescued five Indian chiefs who had
been tortured and staked out to die, and burned down the
settlement.

When he returned to the harbour Raleigh found, to
his immense relief, that two of his ships had arrived. He
could now proceed with his expedition into the interior
of the mainland. First, however, he entertained the
captured Berrio as an honoured guest, asking him all
manner of searching questions about the land and its
inhabitants.

Berrio was philosophic. He knew that one unco-
operative Spanish prisoner could not prevent this keen
and determined Englishman from going where he wished.
He answered Raleigh's questions honestly, and they
talked for a long time. Berrio spoke candidly of the
dangers in this mysterious new world, perhaps even
exaggerating them a little.

He warned Raleigh that the course of the river, lying
through equatorial jungles, was a green hell, and that
monsters never seen before lay along its shores. Everywhere were the Indians, who hated the Spaniards.

But Raleigh was not a Spaniard, and he had the five
tortured chiefs, bandaged and cared for, to confirm this!
He sent out men to sound the mouths of the Orinoco,
and they came back with the word that no channel was
deep enough to take an ocean-going ship. So he ordered

his shallow-draught gallego to be stripped. Her upper works were removed, and her hull was re-equipped as a galley for rowers. In this, and in a barge and two wherries, Raleigh and a hundred men set out up the river with provisions for a month. They moved cautiously, wonderingly, in constant amazement at what they saw.

It took them fifteen days to reach the great broad river. In the distance they could glimpse the clifflike ridge of the plateau. Beyond the plateau rose the mountains of Venezuela, where they were sure they would find the golden city, El Dorado.

None of them was really prepared for this mysterious and elusive world, or the life that it thrust upon them. It fascinated and terrified and drew them on as though they were under a spell. The river itself moved sluggish and secret with more streams and branches than these sailors had seen before. To take the wrong one might lead to the wanderings of a lifetime.

Their Indian guide, Ferdinando, was as bewildered as the strangers. He went ashore to try and unravel the mystery, and there he was captured. Raleigh promptly seized an old Indian and threatened to kill him if Ferdinando were not released. Though Ferdinando managed to escape by his own energy, the old man remained with them as a kind of auxiliary.

The Indians, however, succeeded in cutting only a small hole through the jungle. The tropical sun, the dense forests where no breeze stirred, and the shortage of food raised problems that no man could resolve. Day by day Raleigh had to lighten his men's spirits; not one day was free of the burning anxiety that fresh food—and El Dorado—might elude them.

They were a gallant lot on the whole, and when they could catch fish they were willing to follow their admiral anywhere. But fear was a terrible thing. One day the old Indian led them up a stream so narrow that they had to hack their way with swords—and terror came on one and all. They threatened to kill the old man for

having led them into a trap. Then like a miracle the
stream widened, the branches lifted, and they saw "the
most beautiful country that ever our eyes beheld."

It was a paradise, and remained a paradise until one
of the men went into the river to bathe. Right before
the eyes of his companions, he was eaten by a crocodile.
They shivered but went on, for somewhere within the
compass of this cruel beauty lay the Gilded City.

Small villages were appearing now on the banks of
the river, and the Indians who dwelt there provided the

exploring party with food and cautious friendliness. A day or two later the explorers captured two canoes. In one were three Spaniards, who promptly escaped into the jungle. In the other was a quantity of ore, along with a refiner's basket containing quicksilver, saltpetre, and equipment for panning gold. Their spirits soared.

On, on, they urged each other—to the west where the sky was as gold as their hopes!

They had now penetrated nearly three hundred miles beyond the mouth of the Orinoco. The Indian villages were more and more frequent. To the Indians these men were a marvel. The Spaniards had told them that Englishmen were cannibals, but Raleigh spoke to them courteously and treated them like men.

Even more remarkable to the Indians was the unfailing respect shown to their women. The good discipline of his men gratified Raleigh as well, and he seized an advantage from this. He pointed out to the Indians that his men's good conduct was by his mighty Cacique's command. So he "drew them to admire Her Majesty," and he claimed the land in her name.

It was this mutual trust and respect that opened many secrets to Raleigh. The Indians gave him the remedy for the poison used on their arrows and confirmed his expectation of gold. They gave names to many of the dazzling birds and strange animals, and to that "princess of fruits," the pineapple.

Raleigh, the poet and scientist, was supremely happy. Although gold was his objective, the beauty of the country fed his imagination. This Guiana that he had dreamed of for so many years became the home of his spirit.

The chief cacique of all this land was one hundred and ten years old, and his name was Topiawari. He had suffered greatly from the Spanish.

He and Raleigh talked together as friends. He supplied the English with food; and his son, Caworako, went with Raleigh toward the mountains of Guiana, their journey's end.

Caworako told Raleigh strange tales of a race of men called Ewaipanoma, whose eyes grew in their shoulders and whose mouths lay in the centre of their breasts. Raleigh could scarcely believe him, but Caworako swore that an Ewaipanoma had been seized not twelve months before, and that the club he wielded was the mightiest in the world.

A remarkable magic world, but also a jealous world, guarded by the spirits of the jungle. And the jungle mocked the Englishmen when the rains came, flooding the land. The river rose and drove them back as far as Topiawari's village.

This was so bitter a blow that Raleigh could scarcely believe it. He cheered himself by saying that they could press on again as soon as the rains ceased. But the old chief told him sadly that even when the rainy season was over, the problems of establishing English settlements in this region would be impossible with the number of men he had. The Spaniards had tried, with a larger number, and failed.

As for El Dorado, was gold worth perishing for?

"Go home," he said to Raleigh, "gather a small army, come back. You are an honourable man, and we will not forget you. Many tribes will join because you have not carried off their women and children. But they must see that you are stronger than the Spanish."

For the moment Raleigh was defeated — but only for the moment. He bowed to the old chief's knowledge, and said he would return in a year.

But he could not leave without one last effort. He sent out two reconnaissance parties, one to make its way overland toward the mountains, the other to prospect the streams for samples of gold-bearing rocks. He himself proceeded up the tributary called the Caroni to see if the falls could be climbed and the escarpment reached from this direction.

He soon learned that nothing could be accomplished with his small force.

With knives and bare hands the prospectors did manage to scrabble out some samples of gold-bearing ore for sceptics at home in England. Returning to the Orinoco, they were once more hurled onto its flood-waters.

They steered a drenched and desperate course and they fought each moment for survival. Yet by skill or destiny, Raleigh lost only one man on the whole voyage — the poor fellow who had been eaten by the crocodile.

Leave-takings were filled with tears and dread. Many of the Indians implored him to be faithful to the alliance he had offered, and they made their vows to a queen who would protect them from the hated Spanish. They clung to his hands, promising faithfulness forever. He was deeply moved. He said his greatest hope was to return with his wife and child, and make this land a safe and prosperous place. Next year . . . next year. . . . How could he know that he would not return for twenty years? Or how could he know that for two hundred years his name would live there as a legend?

Two of his men decided to remain: Francis Sparrow to study and sketch the topography, and Hugh Goodwin to study the languages. Chief Topiawari offered them his protection and friendship, and Raleigh took with him to England one of Topiawari's sons, who was there christened with the name the Spaniards gave to Raleigh, "Gualtero."

Raleigh had many doubts about his welcome at home, for the holds of his ships did not carry the gold and jewels which, to eager investors, were the only legitimate proof of success.

He made one last anxious effort, as they passed through the delta, to collect some evidence with which to buy himself a welcome at home. He sent his trusted friend, Lawrence Keymis, to track down the rumours of a gold mine.

Keymis brought back assurance from the Indians that such a gold mine did exist, but the weather was so threatening they did not dare plunge again into the jungle to see with their own eyes.

To Raleigh and his men, the land was rich with promise. They had fallen in love with its sun, its beautiful fruit, its friendly people. But this love could not be translated into the profitable rewards required at home.

Raleigh had set his heart on visiting the colony in Virginia, which had been left to its own survival. It hung about his conscience But terrible storms along the coast forced him to turn back at the Florida Keys.

His future now depended on how persuasively he could convince the Queen that a part of English greatness lay in Guiana, and how well he could reassure his investors that a further expedition would be fool-proof

His reception was as cool as he expected. Only his wife and small son were really glad to see him. He was still not welcome at Court, so he went with his family to Sherborne to await developments.

"Where is the gold?" was the question he was constantly being asked. "Every dolt and gull must be satisfied," he wrote angrily. His enemies made sure that his failure was big enough for all the world to see.

The attacks and the rumours grew Raleigh listened, and wondered what to do He asked Cecil for advice Cecil and his father did what they could, but they were both cautious men

For the Queen, Raleigh had precious and unusual stones cut in rare ways. But whatever value they had in her eyes was offset by the report of a bribed official of the Mint, who declared that Raleigh's gold ore was worthless.

The rumours reached a climax when it was whispered that he had never left England but had been in hiding — that the gold and the jewels came from North Africa

Raleigh was cynical enough about his fellow humans not to be too much surprised by these attacks. He had been working on his answer. It took the form of one of the greatest and most beautiful travel classics of all time, *The Discovery of the Large, Rich, and Beautiful Empire of Guiana.* With brilliance and vividness he made the country come alive. With fresh and loving eyes he showed the reader its peoples, birds, and beasts.

The book was widely read, but there is no evidence that it succeeded in doing what Raleigh desperately hoped it would do; namely, to reinstate him in power, spur his countrymen into establishing more colonies abroad, and send him back to the New World. Most Englishmen — including Elizabeth — had not yet grasped the political and economic importance of colonies. In this, Raleigh was ahead of his time.

6
Singeing the Beard of the Spanish King

One positive development did come out of the Guiana expedition. As a seaman, Raleigh could no longer be overlooked.

In 1596 it was decided that England would send a fleet against her old enemy, Spain. The expedition was to be a mighty undertaking under the joint command of the Lord Admiral, Charles Howard, and Essex. Howard admired Raleigh's seamanship and appointed him Rear Admiral in command of a squadron. Raleigh threw himself into the enterprise with enthusiasm. A blow at Spain was a blow for the protection of Guiana.

An English fleet of ninety-six ships was authorised. The Dutch added twenty-four more, only too glad to be given the chance to strike at their overlord, the King of Spain. The plans also called for a landing force of ten thousand men, to be organised under Sir Francis Vere.

To Raleigh fell the main responsibility for recruiting the ships' crews and supplies. The task was not easy. In spite of his fame as a sea captain, he found that men were no more eager to give their lives to this war than to any other. He wrote to Cecil, "As fast as we press men one day, they come away another and say they will not serve." With his boots crusted with mud, and his elegant clothing torn and dirty, he hunted after runaway mariners and dragged himself in the mire from alehouse to alehouse.

But when he finally arrived at Plymouth to join the other commanders, he had more recruits than he had expected. In Plymouth he also discovered—from the astonishing amount of gold and silver lace on the officers' uniforms—that this campaign was being given the highest standing and support.

The officers, proud, arrogant, and infinitely sensitive of place and position, were soon quarrelling among themselves. Raleigh tried to hold aloof, but he was drawn into an angry exchange with Sir Francis Vere over their spheres of authority. Essex intervened sharply, and gave to Raleigh seniority at sea. Vere was to have seniority on land.

After that Raleigh was even more careful, for this campaign meant the whole future to him. A successful outcome would not only protect his dream of the New World but also bring him money and a return to the Queen's favour.

By June 3 this bristling and ferocious fleet of ambitious men sailed out of Plymouth harbour. Within two weeks they stood off Cadiz, the largest port and richest city of Spain

This destination came as a complete surprise to most of the fleet, and to Philip of Spain it meant utter consternation. Probably no secret in spy-ridden Europe had been so well kept.

A council of war aboard Essex' flagship determined the English action—a simple action as they saw it. Cadiz was at the extreme end of a narrow peninsula. Although protected by four fortresses, it was exposed to open waters on the north, south, and west.

Essex and his squadron were to land men beneath the walls of the city and develop their assault from within the city's own defences. The English squadrons of the

Lord Admiral and his brother, together with the single squadron of the Dutch, would then attack the Spanish fleet A smaller squadron under Sir Alexander Clifford was to finish off the galleys. Raleigh would sail close to the shore and prevent the escape of the merchant ships with their priceless booty, which the Queen wanted above all else.

Confronting the English were six Spanish galleons, as well as three frigates that had recently fought Drake at Puerto Rico, three Levant ships, and twenty powerful galleys. In the harbour there were also forty merchant ships loading for New Spain.

Raleigh sailed off to fulfil his assignment, but before dawn Essex and the Lord Admiral were forced to recognise that their plans had become suicidal. The sailing distance to the actual city of Cadiz was farther than they had estimated, and a strong northwest wind sprang up before they reached their destination. Landing boats were tossing wildly in the heavy waves. And now that the element of surprise was gone, the powerful mass of Spanish ships was making up for lost time.

To persist in the landing of men in such a heavy sea was to condemn the men to death by drowning, yet to attempt the seizure of the city by fighting the Spanish galleons was to go counter to all their strategy.

Stubborn and proud, the Lord Admiral refused to change his orders. In growing dismay, his officers watched two boatloads of soldiers drown, in full armour, before their eyes.

At this moment, Raleigh returned. He felt the heavy seas, saw the massed Spanish strength and the impending disaster. He had never been a man to wait on the feelings of others. He promptly ordered his cockboat and, in the swelling sea, forced his way through the landing boats in which the frightened soldiers were being loaded from Essex' flagship. He assumed Essex would agree that the men could not be landed on an "iron coast" in a heavy sea and a high wind. Instead the English must use both sea and wind to sail into the galleons, batter and then board them.

In great nervous excitement, Essex referred Raleigh to the Lord Admiral. He promised his full support, however, if Raleigh's plan would save them from such "a helpless death at sea."

So Raleigh went his tossing way to the Lord Admiral's ship For his pains he might very well get nothing but a quick arrest and the brig. But one of the strongest elements in Raleigh's character was his calm assumption that he was right in a crisis. He had the ability to disregard most of the unimportant factors, such as a narrow pride or a wounded self-esteem. He usually saw matters realistically, and acted with a sharp independence.

In the present situation he fully expected that the murderous nature of their orders would be plain to all. And sure enough, he found the Lord Admiral confused and unhappy, seeing disaster before him. With obvious relief, Howard revoked his orders.

Once more Raleigh was rowed back to Essex' ship. There the tall Earl and his officers leaned far over the bulwarks, shouting for word. Raleigh did not pause. He called out in Spanish, "We won!" Essex' men shouted their pleasure, and the Earl danced a few steps and tossed his plumed hat into the sea.

A full day and too many lives had already been lost. That night a new council of war was held. With the lights of the city glimmering across the waters, Raleigh's advice prevailed. He was instructed to formulate the orders which would put the English fleet at the mouth of the harbour, where they could attack at dawn. The situation was an extraordinary one. Raleigh, a subordinate officer, was now virtually in command.

He was given the honour of leading the attack in his *Warspite*. Both Essex, so jealous of Raleigh, and the Lord Admiral, so very careful of his position, had stepped aside.

With the first glimpse of day, Raleigh launched the

attack. The merchant ships hurried, as fast as the wind would take them, to anchoring points out of the range of battle. The huge Spanish galleons and men-of-war that made up the main line of defence swung into positions in a narrow neck between two forts, southeast of the city. Raleigh drove his squadron straight at the four famous galleons named for apostles — the *St. Philip, St. Andrew, St. Matthew,* and *St. Thomas.*

The Spanish greeted this bold flying move with a roar of batteries from the shore and a hail of shot from the galleys in the outer bay. The range was too long. A scornful Raleigh greeted each fusillade with a fanfare of trumpets.

A general action of the fleet began, directed primarily against the stately apostolic ships which filled the neck of the channel. The galleys slipped away to join the rest of the Spanish fleet. Raleigh then realised that the firing power lay with the Spaniards. Their broadside guns were unimpeded, whereas he could use only his bow pieces.

It now became obvious that the various commanding officers of the English fleet were all manoeuvering for the best position. The channel became so crowded with English ships striving for a place of glory that the flyboats, to which the task of boarding the galleons was assigned, could not get into position.

Essex thrust up his flagship through the squadron and anchored next to Raleigh. Furious, he accused Raleigh of being brave at a distance. Raleigh was equally furious at being put in such a position that his *Warspite* took a pounding. He had himself quickly rowed to Essex' ship, threatening to disregard orders and hazard a Queen's ship if the flyboats were delayed any longer. "It was the same loss," he said, "to burn or sink."

Essex, in the excitement of battle, could be a good commander. He promised that he would endorse whatever move Raleigh made. But Raleigh still had the ambition of the other commanders to contend with. During the

fifteen minutes he had been absent from his ship, Sir Francis Vere had squeezed ahead of Raleigh's ship. Then Thomas Howard, brother of the Lord Admiral, had squeezed ahead of Vere.

Raleigh, seeing the manoeuvre, slipped past Vere to reach the vantage point in the channel. Vere tried to out-manoeuvre him by secretly getting a hawser or large rope aboard Raleigh's ship and so drawing his own closer. But Raleigh ordered his friend's hawser chopped off without delay. He then changed the arrangement of

his squadron and drove his own ship alongside the great
St. Philip. Essex and Lord Thomas Howard brought him
their support.

The four great galleons soon gave up the fight. Two
were driven by their crew into shallow waters, and all
four burst into flames. At this point all Spanish resist-
ance began to collapse. Pandemonium followed.

"Many drowned themselves," Raleigh later wrote.
"Many half-burnt, leaped into the water; very many,
hanging by the ropes-ends by the ship's sides were under

the water even to the lips; many swimming with grievous wounds were stricken under water and put out of their pain; and withal, so huge a fire and such tearing of the ordnance of the great *Philip* and the rest (that) if any man had desire to see hell itself, it was there most lively figured. Ourselves spared the lives of all after the victory; but the Dutch who did little or nothing in the fight, used merciless slaughter, till they were by myself, and after my Lord Admiral, beaten off."

As the carnage rose to a climax, Raleigh fell. His leg was so splintered that he would have rolled into the sea in his agony had his men not held him back.

The sack of the great city followed. Exhilarated almost beyond reason by the English shouts of triumph, Raleigh ordered himself carried ashore and even tried to mount a horse. But his pain and weakness were too great. He was forced to return to his ship, where he tossed in a furious fever.

The English commanders forbade violence to civilians under pain of death. Even the Spanish king praised the victors' conduct.

The spoils were enormous. Many leading Spaniards were seized and held for ransom. A ransom was demanded for the city itself.

The merchant ships, huddled in a safe estuary, carried cargoes valued at eight million ducats. Raleigh asked permission to seize these great prizes of war. But his senior officers, struggling to bring order out of chaos, did not hear his request until too late. At the end of the day, someone looked toward the east and saw great columns of smoke rising against the sky. The Spanish commanders had set fire to the merchant ships and so snatched from the English the prize they valued most.

On July 3, after fierce debate over the fate of Cadiz, Essex and the Lord Admiral decided to evacuate the city. The fleet turned toward home. "Many rich prisoners were given to the land commanders . . . some held prisoners for 16,000 ducats, some for twenty thousand, some for ten thousand; beside great houses of merchandise. For my own part, I have got a game leg and deformed. I have possession of naught but poverty and pain."

In these words Raleigh expressed his bitterness. In actual fact, he did have some material rewards. His share of the booty was £1,769. And the other commanders, jealous though they were of their own honour, were exceptionally generous in their praise of him. Moreover, the long rivalry with Essex seemed to be laid at rest.

Essex had what he wanted. To the people of London, he was now a hero. They cheered him whenever he appeared on the street. The Queen watched but showed no special signs of favour. Indeed she complained as bitterly as Raleigh that men and officers had plundered her proper share of the Cadiz booty.

But Robert Cecil showed an unexpected warmth to Essex, and his favour could not be underestimated. During Essex' absence, Cecil had been made First Secretary.

That winter of 1596—97, Cecil, Essex, and Raleigh dined constantly together. Many observed this with great amazement and some dismay. No three men could be more different, yet such a powerful triumvirate called up the memory of Mark Antony, Octavius Caesar, and Lepidus, who had divided the rule of the Roman world among themselves.

7

An Ill-Fated
Expedition

The wilful and aging Queen, for her part, was apparently
grateful that Raleigh, Essex, and Cecil were joined in
friendship. She seems not to have feared any attempt
on their part to seize power, perhaps because she understood the three so well. She loved Essex, and now saw
him the hero of London and Master of the Ordnance,
which meant commander in chief of the military forces
within the country. She admired Raleigh, whom she
had punished for five years and now permitted to return
to Court as Captain of the Guard. She needed Cecil, and
made him Chancellor of the Duchy of Lancaster as well
as her First Secretary.

All were happy, but it was the quiet before a storm.

Philip of Spain, though dying from a painful illness,
was obsessed by the need to revenge himself for the
sack of Cadiz. His treasuries were exhausted and his
country nearly bankrupt, yet he swore that he would
pawn all his possessions rather than forsake his revenge.
Scarcely able to move with the pain of his illness, he
kept himself alive by making and unmaking plans.

Raleigh, Essex, and Cecil were all convinced that
the only way to settle the whole matter was by attack.

Attack the Spanish fleet in its port at Ferrol, and then go on to trap the West Indies treasure fleet, which was Philip's last hope in the New World.

The Queen, for perhaps the first time in her cautious life, agreed.

Raleigh was granted the contract to provision the fleet. Essex was chief in command, and Lord Thomas Howard was Vice-Admiral. Raleigh, as Rear-Admiral, commanded his old squadron.

Terrible storms broke out before the English ever reached Spain. Their ships reeled this way and that. Masts cracked, seams sprang open. Raleigh kept his squadron together by one means or another and tried to push on to Finisterre. But the gales were so shattering that the bulkheads of the *Warspite* were broken and her cookroom smashed. He headed back to Plymouth. Essex also turned back, his ship barely afloat by the time he reached England.

Only Lord Thomas succeeded in struggling to the Spanish coast where, torn and encrusted with salt spray, his squadron roared its defiance while waiting for the others. But the Spanish refused to be tempted even by this battered remnant of the English flotilla. Lord Thomas finally had no choice but to take himself home.

There he found Raleigh and Essex preparing for a second attempt. In August of 1597 the ships were ready to start out again.

On this new voyage Essex could not make up his mind on anything. He wavered, his orders shifted. As commander in chief, he looked for signs in the heavens to tell him what to do. He listened to every rumour. He trusted no one, yet trusted all.

A storm off the Portuguese coast broke Raleigh's mainyard and sprang a leak in Essex' flagship. Essex pushed on to the Azores, where he waited for Raleigh's arrival.

A council of war then determined that the English squadrons should spread out and cover the central group of the Azores. But Essex, still responding to every rumour, kept changing the orders. At length, under great pressure from Raleigh, he reverted to his original orders. Then he became so impatient to carry them out that at midnight he abruptly sent a message to Raleigh to follow him without delay to Fayal, the chief island of the Azores.

Raleigh promptly obeyed, though he was seriously short of water. The next morning when he and his ships entered the roads of Fayal, there was no sign of Essex. Raleigh and his men were amazed and disquieted but there was nothing to do but cast anchor and wait. When the Spanish forts opened fire, Raleigh's men implored him to fight. He refused, even though his pride was greatly troubled by the thought that the islanders would think him afraid. He was well aware (and Essex' followers did not let him forget) that the commander in chief wished the glory of the first attack.

For three days Raleigh waited, watching the Spanish strengthen their defences along the shore. At last, on the fourth day, his patience broke, and his own desire for glory overcame him. When his boats, seeking water, were fired upon, he abruptly landed two hundred and sixty soldiers and sailors on a rocky beach. Although lamed by the wound received at Cadiz, he shouted scornfully that those who were not afraid should follow him. He jumped into the surf from the landing boat and led a handful of officers into a withering fire.

When Raleigh called for further volunteers, Essex' friends held back. Raleigh very nearly stripped his own ships of men in order to hold the beachhead. Wearing only the piece of armour which covered his throat, he limped across the field of fire, aided by his cane. His cousin, Sir Arthur Gorges, suffered a burned leg from a musket ball, and Raleigh's clothes were torn by bullets. But when Raleigh suggested that Gorges take off the red scarf he was wearing, Gorges retorted that Raleigh's white scarf was as good a target as his red one.

Neither would honour the Spanish marksmen by altering his dress or his course. And eventually they took the hill.

The next day Raleigh's lookouts spied the sails of Essex' ships. The Earl had gone off on a wild chase without signalling to his fleet, and he was now astounded to find that Raleigh had taken action. Raleigh's enemies lost no time in urging Essex to court-martial him.

When Raleigh climbed aboard the *Du Repulse* expecting to be praised by Essex for an English victory, he found himself in deadly danger. But Raleigh had learned much during his months of friendship with Essex. He did not defend himself. He said there was nothing to defend. He was third in order of command, and when both Essex and Lord Thomas Howard were absent from the rendezvous, the charge fell to him.

Essex' expression cleared. Seizing Raleigh's hand, he exclaimed, "You are right!"

The Earl could now hardly wait to inspect the landings. He praised all he saw and eagerly accepted Raleigh's invitation to dinner aboard the *Warspite*.

But that night Raleigh's enemies took care to show Essex that Raleigh had made the only positive move in the whole expedition. An astute queen would know whom to reward. At the same time, Raleigh's friends warned him of a recurrence of danger. Raleigh made plans to fight Essex with his squadron if Essex tried to arrest him.

It was Lord Thomas who intervened. Lord Thomas was no friend of Raleigh, but he had some good sense. He persuaded Essex to accept an apology from Raleigh, and then he had himself rowed to Raleigh's ship. As a good seaman, he said, he knew that Raleigh had acted correctly, but Essex' wounded vanity was a formidable danger to their success. "Let us be realistic; apologise and all will be well."

Raleigh, a hard-headed man, was exceedingly wary of trusting himself aboard his friend's flagship, but

Lord Thomas guaranteed his safety. Raleigh came aboard the flagship with full ceremony, and Essex formally censured him. Raleigh apologised. Essex accepted the apology. Raleigh dined with Essex on the *Due Repulse,* and then Essex was rowed to dine with Raleigh on the *Warspite.*

After all this formal nonsense had been completed, they again turned their attention to the Spaniards. Raleigh urged that the attack, so long delayed, be mounted instantly. Everyone hurried into action only to find that the Spanish had fled. Essex' men were furious that Raleigh had let live ransom slip through his fingers. Raleigh's men retorted that none of this would have happened if the Earl had given his prompt support rather than wasting time on all the disciplinary foolishness.

They burned the city and sailed away with no ransom and no prizes.

Essex was now determined to throw out the long-delayed net of ships and draw in the treasure fleet. He gave his orders, countermanded them, and then to his horror discovered that his first orders — if executed — would have caught the treasure fleet.

Essex was out of his mind with chagrin. He had no one to blame but himself. He had veered in all directions like a weathercock. Several of his powerful officers were even beginning to wonder whether they had better not cut adrift from this unstable man.

The high climax of futility was reached when the fleet finally straggled back into Plymouth. There they learned that, on the very day they had set sail for home, an armada of one hundred and thirty-six Spanish ships had sailed for England. The Spanish planned to meet the straggling and unsuspecting fleet of Essex near the coast of England. Only the capricious winds had intervened and blown the Spanish off their course so that the English fleet had not even seen the great enemy net of ships.

The returning Englishmen were thoroughly chastened and subdued. They realised, as did all of England, that the danger from this new fleet had been far greater than the danger in 1588 when the first armada had appeared.

Raleigh lost his rank of rear admiral, and his career as a regular naval commander came to an end. He did not specially care. He hated the sea. But Essex' reputation suffered a much more severe blow. For him the disaster marked the beginning of his downfall.

8
Climax of Rivalry

Elizabeth did not seem to hold the ill-fated Islands Voyage against Raleigh. Indeed, his advice was constantly sought by both Queen and Council. Many said that Walter Raleigh had again become her first favourite.

But Raleigh himself was not lulled into any false security. During the next quiet years, he built his defences, skilfully, increased his enormous wealth, and began the education of his son Wat. He loved this boy very much, and tried to give to him some of his own wide learning and vivid interest in the world. Wat was a wild-tempered boy, intelligent, spoiled — trying to imitate his father in everything.

Raleigh also returned to Parliament, and his home in London — Durham House — became an important political centre in the city. There, too, his world-wide interests found their full expression. He had kept alive his interest in the New World in as many ways as he could. Now he worked hard at making the tobacco imported from Virginia popular among the English, for this would benefit the settlements in Virginia.

Bess Raleigh disliked Durham House because from the study her husband could see the tall ships below

London Bridge. She dreaded the longing look in his eyes. There were rumours that Raleigh was organising another voyage to Guiana, and he did send at least one small ship to let the natives there know that he had not forgotten them.

When Essex was eventually restored to partial favour at Court, Raleigh avoided him as much as he could. Their friendship had become more and more strained, and Raleigh wanted to keep away from political entanglements. His dream of being a member of the Privy Council had never been realised; there was little chance of it now.

The Queen was old. She was well aware that almost everyone at Court was speculating on her successor, but it was a subject she forbade in her hearing. She did not want to die. To talk of a successor was to talk of her death.

Yet a peaceful change of sovereigns was on everyone's mind, and most Englishmen believed that their next ruler would be James VI, King of Scotland and a cousin of Queen Elizabeth. Cecil was in constant secret correspondence with him. Every powerful man, and some not so powerful, were trying in secret ways to win favour with James. Raleigh sometimes seemed the only man of power who remained aloof. He did not know that his old friend Cecil was warning James of him. Nor did he know that James had been wondering why Raleigh, the Captain of the Guard, and the most influential man at Court, had not sent him a letter.

Essex was flamboyantly and imprudently a partisan of James, and James was responding with a hearty good will.

In Ireland, meanwhile, trouble and unrest were increasing. Essex saw it as a desperate last chance to restore his reputation. Elizabeth wavered, not trusting his skill against the great Earl of Tyrone, who was leading the Irish rebels. Rumours everywhere said that Raleigh would be put in command. But in the end the

Queen gave Essex what he wanted.

After a triumphant ride through London, where the people who loved him sent up cheer after cheer, Essex set out for Ireland with a force of more than 17,000 men. It was the largest army to leave English shores during Elizabeth's reign.

Essex carried specific instructions from the Queen, but the moment he reached Ireland he put them aside in order to embark on a programme of peacemaking. With a large retinue, he travelled about the countryside like a prince. The Queen sent him a furious message telling him that such displays were costing her a thousand pounds a day. And she had nothing to show in return but raging Irish clansmen. This threw Essex into a fury. He wrote an angry reply, blaming Raleigh for all his misfortunes.

There is no proof that Raleigh worked against him. But Essex became obsessively convinced that Raleigh was his enemy with constant access to the Queen. Having fritted away his chances for waging a successful campaign, he begged the Queen to allow him to return home. But she refused — without a victory. He then took matters into his own hands. Without warning he returned to England and came riding furiously into London. Spattered with mud, he broke into the Queen's apartments. He threatened her, and then he wept. Under the circumstances of his defiance, there was little the Queen could do but put him under arrest.

The Court and London were clamorous with excitement. Essex' popularity with the people was legendary. The Queen, under public pressure, released him, but she did not allow him to come to Court.

Now Essex' obsession gnawed at him day and night. He sent secret envoys to the King of Scotland and to his old friend Lord Mountjoy, who had succeeded him in Ireland. His actions became so erratic and suspicious that at length the Privy Council ordered him to appear before them. He refused, claiming he was sick.

Raleigh, as Captain of the Guard, knew each step that must be taken. To him fell the task of emissary. He asked that his cousin, Ferdinando Gorges, a fanatical admirer of Essex, meet him at Durham House to set forth Essex' grievances.

Essex refused to allow Gorges to go to Durham House, but agreed to a meeting in the middle of the Thames.

There, swaying in their boats, Raleigh and Gorges talked fruitlessly. Four shots fired at Raleigh from the direction of Essex House put a sudden end to the conference. Gorges left the river in some haste, while Raleigh returned to the Queen to set in motion his grimmer duties.

At midday Essex and two hundred followers poured out of Essex House, shouting that they must save the Queen from Raleigh and her foes. The people of London who loved Essex were bewildered. What did he want of them? Armed revolt? That they could not give. He pleaded with passers-by. At length shots were exchanged and Essex and his friends fought with the Queen's militia. In less than an hour, insurrection had been raised, men had been killed, and Essex was in flight.

He managed to reach his palace by the riverside, and there he barricaded himself with his wife, sister, and those followers who remained with him.

By nightfall the palace was under siege by land and river, surrounded with troops. At length, by the light of torches, Essex could be seen walking on the roof of his palace. There, with a gesture of farewell to the city, he made his surrender.

It was a terrible, glittering downfall. This young man of such surpassing appearance, daring mind, and dazzling personality from whose own follies the Queen had repeatedly protected him — had sought and found an end which was almost as dazzling as himself. All London mourned, for few could resist his charm.

That night Raleigh's name was cursed. In the minds of the people, he had acquired a power malignant enough to pull down their golden youth.

But it was not Raleigh — or even Cecil as rumour claimed — who had pulled him down. It was the Queen herself who could not in the end tolerate his great follies which were a threat to her sovereignty.

Essex' trial began in February, 1601. Dressed in black, he moved with proud disdain. The prosecuting attorney, Essex' old friend Francis Bacon, and the Attorney General, Edward Coke, had little to do but present the factual charges. These they embellished with their own ambitions.

Through all the testimony, Raleigh's name ran like a theme in music. *Raleigh — Raleigh — Raleigh — that fox* — as though Essex had no other enemies. But at length under Cecil's persistent questions, one conspirator scornfully admitted that neither he nor Essex really believed that Raleigh intended them harm.

The final verdict was death — death by beheading.

Up to the last moment, few believed that the Queen would let Essex die. But though she wept and her despair was great, she did not raise her hand to save him.

Essex came out to die dressed as splendidly as though going to Court. He bore himself with great composure and confessed that he had been his own worst enemy.

As Captain of the Guard, Raleigh was obliged to witness the execution. But feeling that his presence would be cruelly painful to Essex, he withdrew to a window overlooking the block.

He was to regret it later. For when Essex asked for him in order that they might be reconciled, Raleigh could not be found. Later when he returned to his own home, many people noticed the sadness on his face.

Essex' descent was final.

Would Raleigh now rise to the height?

9

A New Sovereign

The death of Essex unleashed storms of uneasiness. In taverns and streets, songs were sung in his memory. He became the great Protestant champion of Europe, while Raleigh — linked to his downfall — by some twist of logic became the friend of Spain. Could anything be more ironic?

Raleigh cared nothing for the opinions of a crowd. Essex' easy and dramatic ways had never been Raleigh's ways. He seemed completely indifferent to what people thought of him. In all his years at Court, he had never lost his quick, blunt way of speaking. He lived from day to day, seeming to take no special thought for the future. Elizabeth was his queen. The present was enough for him.

More than ever he loved the excitement of new problems to conquer, new ideas to explore. He loved his wife, who was his most steadfast friend, and his son, who was as lively and questioning as he had been when a boy. He was made Governor of Jersey, a position which carried no money but much work. And in Parliament he became an even greater force than in the past. Everyone expected that he would be made a lord — an earl, perhaps. With a peerage he could accumulate more power and riches. Raleigh did not know that his good friend Cecil had secretly intervened to prevent this, just as he had managed to shift the blame for Essex' execution on to Raleigh.

Cecil was beginning to see in Raleigh a dangerous threat to his own future. He was already warning James in Scotland of "these gaping crabs (Raleigh especially)." . . . "Raleigh, the most dangerous to your crown in England . . . able to sway all men's courses." Cecil told James that Henry Brooke (Lord Cobham), Cecil's brother-in-law and a close friend of Raleigh's, had repeated in artless gossip all the scornful things Raleigh had said of James. The First Secretary assured James that he was cleverly using the two men to their own defeat, by writing to Cobham "as his loving relative" and to Raleigh as his "faithful friend who showed extra-ordinary care for his well-being."

How could Raleigh suspect this kind of treachery? To him Cecil was not only a trustworthy man but a trusted friend. Cecil's son Will had lived with the Raleighs for years at a time, and had been loved almost as much as their own Wat.

Why did Cecil do it? The simplest explanation is perhaps the truest. James had always been known to fancy handsome and splendid men. Raleigh was such a man; Cecil was not. Cecil was determined, for good reasons and bad, to remain what Elizabeth had made him — First Secretary. The only man who offered any threat was Raleigh.

Were James left unwarned, unalarmed — were he to see the man in all his handsome splendour — he would probably find him irresistible.

So Cecil set to work. Because James was deeply re-ligious Cecil, in his letters, charged Raleigh with being an atheist. Because James loathed the use of tobacco, "a vile and stinking custom," Cecil pointed out that Raleigh was responsible for its use in England. Most important, he asked why Raleigh, as Captain of the Guard, the foremost man at Court, had not made overtures to James?

Cecil closed one letter to James: "I will . . . leave the best and worst of him, and other things, to 3." The number 3 was the code for Lord Henry Howard, who often acted as a secret agent in the exchange of correspondence between Cecil and James. Henry Howard, a distant kinsman of the Lord Admiral, had good reasons to hate the Tudor rulers. His father had been put to death by Henry VIII, and his brother had been beheaded for treason by Queen Elizabeth. Raleigh's close association with the Queen made him a logical target for Howard's jealousy. He had no enemy more bitter.

Howard said Raleigh was a man "who in pride exceedeth all men alive—a pride above the greatest Lucifer that hath lived in our age." . . . Raleigh was deft, subtle, evil; it was he who inspired the weak and susceptible Cobham with his own passions, but both were very dangerous. . . . So Howard distilled his poison.

Even Bess was attacked. *She,* according to Howard, was the dominating influence at "the evil sessions" held in Durham House, where "witchcraft was practiced." James hated witches.

Raleigh knew nothing of this. His superb self-assurance was both his friend and his enemy. His inability to conceal his contempt for artifice and policy made him hated by devious men. If a bill in Parliament, desired by the Queen, seemed to his keen mind an abuse of power, he said so, and fought it.

He was seldom tactful. He said what he felt—even his courtesy was often ironic. Men generally knew exactly where they stood with him, and this could be a refreshing experience in an age of double-dealing. But the more the King of Scotland heard of the brilliant, versatile, and independent Raleigh, the more his nervous suspicions saw in Raleigh a sinister threat.

During the winter of 1603 the aging Elizabeth fell
ill with a severe cold. Realising that she had not long
to live, she approved James of Scotland as her successor.
Then on March 24 she died. Relays of horses and men
had been stationed from London to Scotland so that
James might know, without delay, when he was king of
England. His succession was immediately proclaimed.

James started toward London. His journey was leis-
urely. Many Englishmen, careful for their future,
rushed to greet him, and he created so many new knights
that it grew to be a joke. At length he issued a pro-

clamation forbidding any man to approach him unless authorised.

Such a proclamation meant nothing to Raleigh. It would never have occurred to him that such a restriction was intended for a man in his position. On the other hand, it *had* occurred to him, somewhat belatedly, that he had better present himself to his new sovereign.

He came unannounced, unauthorised, to this bumbling, shapeless new king. Cecil had done his work so carefully that James saw the handsome, graceful man as merely a sinister affront to himself. He looked at him angrily. His greeting was a wretched pun on Raleigh's name.

"Raleigh, Raleigh! On my soul, mon, I have heard *rawlȳ* of thee."

It was quickly reported to Cecil that Raleigh had "failed to take root."

But *Cecil* took root. Cecil became indispensable. Within two months he mounted the ladder of nobility — first as a baron, then a viscount, and last, as the Earl of Salisbury and First Secretary to the King.

Within four months, Raleigh was stripped of all he possessed and stood in deadly danger of his life.

As the blows came, Raleigh scarcely fought them. Long ago he had taken his own measure, and a curious unworldliness determined his dealings with others.

When James took from him his position as Captain of the Guard, Raleigh made a little joke. But when James ordered him to leave Durham House — his home for twenty years — within two weeks, Raleigh could not make a joke of that. He protested that "the poorest artificer hath a quarter's warning given him by his landlord."

In July the King invited Raleigh to Windsor Castle to join him on a hunt. As Raleigh was waiting on the terrace, Cecil came and said that the King wished him to remain for a few questions by the Privy Council.

Before the day was over, he was charged with high treason. By July 20 he was again a prisoner in the Tower.

10
Charged with Treason

Treason had a deathly sound. Indeed the charge, even when unproven, had been responsible for the death of many Englishmen.

It was rare that a new sovereign came to a throne without having to withstand and perhaps survive many plots against his life and reign. Kings expected plots. They also expected that their closest counsellor — whose career depended on the sovereign's safety — should be well aware of every whispered danger.

Cecil, by his temperament, his own sharp intelligence, and his army of spies, was well qualified to know all secrets. He had learned that Spain was prepared to supply money that would topple James off the throne and crown as Queen of England, Arabella Stuart.

Arabella Stuart, descended like James from Henry VII, had an even better claim to the English crown than James. But for various reasons, including her own lack of interest, this claim had never been seriously considered.

Although Arabella knew nothing of the plot, it was assumed that she would do all the plotters wished — make peace with Spain, allow the English Catholics to return to power, and permit herself to be married to whatever prince offered the highest bid.

After Cecil had collected all the details of the plot, he arrested the conspirators, one by one. Nine suspects were taken, among them Lord Cobham and his brother, George Brooke. They confessed everything and involved as many others as they could in an effort to relieve themselves of the greatest blame. One of the men Cobham promptly mentioned was Raleigh.

When Raleigh was first questioned he seemed genuinely bewildered, and he denied that he knew of *any* plot. Then when he realised that confessions were pouring out and the truth — however innocent — could not be concealed, he admitted that Cobham had dangled a pension from Spain before him. In exchange he was to supply secret information.

His enemies seized on this.

First he had denied a plot; now he was admitting it! The man was a traitor!

No man knew better than Raleigh the small likelihood of justice. His only chance lay in gaining some support for himself, and in fighting shrewdly. Both had to be done in the dark.

Bess, outside the Tower, did all she could. She devotedly carried out his instructions, begging help of Cecil, since neither she nor Raleigh knew the full extent of Cecil's double-dealing. And she encouraged her husband in every way she could. But the heaviest burden of the fight fell on Raleigh himself.

He was questioned in private with practically no chance to know the full charges or to confront his accusers. He was allowed no counsel and had to rely on his own quickness of wit and elementary knowledge of the law. Then he discovered that Cecil, his supposed friend, had tricked Cobham into still another confession by telling Cobham that Raleigh had accused him. A wave of hopelessness swept over Raleigh. If James had resolved on his death, there was little hope of being saved. Judges had lost their offices and juries been penalised for acquitting prisoners whom the sovereign wished convicted.

Raleigh stabbed himself.

Cecil, who was questioning other prisoners, rushed in and found Raleigh in great pain. Raleigh protested that he would rather kill himself than have his innocence doubted. Cecil hurriedly hushed up the event, realising perhaps that it was not a true suicide effort. How could a man as skilled in weapons as Raleigh fail in a simple stabbing? Instead Cecil thought it a desperate effort on Raleigh's part to proclaim his innocence to the world.

Raleigh's trial was set for November 17, 1603. He prepared himself as well as possible. One of his principal tasks was to keep Cobham steady. He must force Cobham to stick to the truth. Raleigh was not allowed to speak to Cobham or exchange letters, but his old friend, Lawrence Keymis, managed to reach Cobham and begged him to speak the truth. Keymis assured Cobham that the law required two witnesses before either he or Raleigh could be condemned.

Then Cobham begged to make a new statement to the Council, but the Lieutenant of the Tower, Sir George Harvey, suppressed the appeal.

When Harvey's own son told Raleigh of this trick, Raleigh had a servant toss an apple, to which was tied a second letter, through Cobham's window. In the letter Raleigh begged him not to endanger either of them by confessions made from fear.

Cobham managed to get back a reply, which Raleigh considered "a very good letter." He put it away for his future use.

In November London was raging with the plague, so the trial was transferred to Winchester, an ancient capital of Britain. Though London was filled with dead and dying, the people flocked out in shrieking hordes to curse at Raleigh—the man who had "killed Essex"—

as he passed under guard in his coach. The ghost of Essex was still powerful.

The mob shook the carriage back and forth and hurled tobacco pipes, stones, and mud at the windows. Inside the carriage Raleigh sat quietly, smoking his pipe. He looked out with that large curiosity and detachment which had made so many enemies for him. There was a kind of awful bravery in his calm, but of course Raleigh's courage had never been criticised, only his vast indifference to public opinion.

They reached Winchester by nightfall. The walled old town was jammed with the curious, as well as with the officials concerned with the trial.

That night Raleigh spent in a frigid cell in Wolversey Castle. When morning came, he hid all his deep concern in a valiant effort to defeat the chill which had eaten in to his bones during the night. His hands were trembling from the cold.

He needed the most dauntless spirit and appearance, for seven of the conspirators had already been tried and condemned to death. The proceedings were ruled by a bench of commissioners, of whom some were lawyers and some were not. There is no legal counterpart for them today. The Chief Justice was supported by three other judges, and a jury of twelve knights rendered the verdict.

Among the commissioners was Lord Thomas Howard, who had fought with Raleigh at Cadiz and both hated and admired him. Then there was Lord Henry Howard, who had written the venomous letters to James and who later admitted that he was the originator of the plot for which Raleigh was being tried. Cecil, who with Henry Howard had done all he could to bring Raleigh to this very place, was another commissioner. And the list also included Sir William Waad, a Privy Council "spy" who had worked hard to trap Raleigh into dangerous admissions under the guise of friendship, and Lord Mountjoy, who had been one of Essex' closest friends.

The Lord Chief Justice, Sir John Popham, was a

unique and sinister figure. He had been kidnapped by gypsies in his childhood and had been a highway robber during his youth, stopping travellers at the point of a gun. When he became a lawyer, he acquired the largest fortune ever held by a member of the English bar. This reputedly was acquired from bribe-taking.

A clerk read the indictment against Raleigh: conspiracy to deprive the King of his government, to raise up sedition, to bring in the Roman Catholic Church as the state religion, and to buy the invasion of foreign enemies.

The particulars were so imaginative and improbable that much lying would be needed to support them. Raleigh pleaded not guilty.

It is said that he smiled frequently through this trial, and indeed he needed some such weapon against the bludgeoning tactics of Sir Edward Coke, the Attorney General. Coke had proclaimed Essex guilty before Essex' trial; he now proclaimed Raleigh's guilt.

Although Coke is admired to this day for his profound knowledge and exposition of the law, he was also a man of an abusive temper. By his behaviour, he often disgraced the law he loved.

Raleigh said an illness in the Tower had affected his memory, which had never been good. Might he reply to questions as they came up, rather than all at once? Coke objected. It would "dismember the King's evidence." But the judges, after much discussion, agreed.

All Raleigh was allowed in the way of defence was ink and paper with which to make notes. He could not speak until given permission to do so, and this permission was almost unobtainable. Coke's opening speech was a tirade against traitors in which he constantly wove in references to "plots," and the wisdom and sweetness of the King. His hode-podge of references would have confused the most careful listener.

Raleigh protested. He asked for proof of these wild charges.

"I will prove all. Thou art a monster!" Coke shouted. "Thou hast an English face but a Spanish heart. Thy will was to seat a false claimant on the throne of England —— "

"That is news to me —— "

"Thou art a viper, a traitor, a monster!"

"To call me names is all that you can do."

"Have I angered you?" Coke asked eagerly.

Raleigh replied with some amusement that whatever temper had been lost did not belong to him. The audience tittered.

Thus the trial went on all day. It was made up of innuendoes, rumours, and falsehoods mixed shrewdly with legal language. Raleigh was left to fight his defence with the only weapon he had — his cool brain and his skilful use of words.

It was a bitterly uneven contest. Yet as an eyewitness later wrote, Raleigh looked not only gallant but gay; and he struck back at these tearing, baying enemies "with that wit, learning, courage, and judgment that, save it went with the hazard of his life, it was the happiest day that ever he spent."

Since Cobham's confession was the heart of the charge against Raleigh, Raleigh had to prove that Cobham was completely unreliable, and bent on his destruction. When Raleigh said simply that Cobham's confession was like "an egg hatched by the moon," all understood that the meant no man in his senses would be taken in.

But Coke twisted the facts so that Cobham seemed the victim of Raleigh's clever tongue. Raleigh tried to keep Coke to the line. "I do not hear yet that you have spoken one word against me. Here is no treason of mine done. If my Lord Cobham be a traitor, what is that to me?"

Coke shouted, "All that he did was by thy instigation, thou viper. I'll prove thee the rankest traitor in all England!"

Raleigh stood very tall above the stocky prosecutor,

whose eyes were described "as hard and glossy as chestnuts."

"No, Mr. Attorney, I am no traitor. Whether I live or die, I shall stand as true a subject as any the King hath."

When Coke, in a frenzy of anger, said, "I want words sufficient to express thy viperous treasons!" Raleigh answered, with an ironic smile, "I think you want words indeed, for you have spoken one thing half a dozen times."

Raleigh's whole manner had changed. He was now calm, at ease, as though the terrible odds against him had roused in him the desire to fight for life itself.

The Lord Chief Justice intervened to balance the matter for Coke. He ordered Cobham's confession read, in which Cobham claimed Raleigh had forced him on to this course.

Raleigh's handsome face showed only scorn, although for prudence he tried to conceal it. Within his own jacket burned the letter in which Cobham wrote so passionately of Raleigh's innocence.

Raleigh requested permission to reply in his own defence. With an understandable contempt he asked why he, who had no power, no importance, should enter a conspiracy *in favour of* Spain, the land which called him "The Old Pirate." And why would he enter a conspiracy at the very moment that Spain's power was waning, "when we have the kingdom of Scotland united, Ireland quieted, Denmark assured, the Low Countries our nearest neighbours. And instead of a Lady whom time hath surprised, we have now an active King who is able to attend to his own business. I am not such a madman as to make myself in this time a Robin Hood. . . ."

Now that he held his listeners, he pressed his points hard, and no one seemed to have the power or wish to interrupt. "Thrice have I served against Spain at sea, wherein for my country's sake, I had expended of my own properties, £4000. I knew that where, before, the King of Spain was wont to have forty great sails at the least in his ports, now he hath not past six or seven; and for sending to his Indies, he is driven to hire strange vessels. And whoso knows well the King of Spain will not think he would so freely disburse to my Lord Cobham 600,000 crowns!"

There was the sound of the sea in his broad Devon accent. To those who listened it recalled those fierce men who had first challenged Spanish power, sent an armada reeling, and turned a small island into a great power.

He then asked for simple justice. "Look, my lords, I claim to have my accuser brought here face to face to speak. . . . I have learned that by the law of this realm, in case of treason, a man ought to be convicted by the testimony of two witnesses if they be living. By the law of God, the life of man is of such price and value that no person ought to die unless he be condemned rightly."

The audience sucked in their breath. He had made a distinction vivid in English minds. The law of God was inherent in the conception of rights, and it took precedence over the laws of men. But the judges still refused him.

Then Raleigh demanded that one accuser, Cobham, charge him to his face.

Again they refused. They would not bring up Cobham, who lay in the cell below the hall.

The damaging, irresponsible charges and the unheeded denials continued until once more Raleigh asked to be confronted with Cobham.

"It is you, Mr. Attorney," he said to Coke, "who should press for his testimony and I who should fear his producing — if all be true that you have alleged."

Cecil unexpectedly supported Raleigh. What were Cecil's thoughts? Why did this cold fish of a man show sudden signs of human feelings toward a man who had been his constant friend for years and whom he had betrayed?

"Could not the proceedings be delayed while the judge ascertained the King's pleasure?" Cecil inquired.

But the judges refused.

Raleigh begged the jury to consider the utter flimsiness of the case against him. He asked them to put themselves in his place — "in hazard of your life . . . upon an accusation not subscribed to by your accuser — without the open testimony of a single witness . . ."

The charges were now hastily summed up. When everything seemed at an end, Raleigh said, "Mr. Attorney, have you done?"

"Yes, if you have no more to say."

"If you have done," Raleigh responded, "then I have somewhat more to say."

"Nay, I will have the last word for the King!"

"No, I will have the last word for my life!"

"Go to," Coke roared, "I will lay thee upon thy back for the greatest traitor that ever came to the bar,"

Again Cecil intervened. "Be not so impatient, good Mr. Attorney. Give him leave to speak."

Coke shook his fist at Raleigh. The spectators hissed. In a rage he sat down, and he would not stand up again until begged by all the commissioners.

But when he rose, Coke produced his trump: an additional "confession" by Cobham. In it he begged forgiveness for his "double-dealings" and charged that Raleigh had demanded £1500 a year as pension from the Spanish government for giving information.

Coke read this confession in a shouting voice. Then he cried, "Now, Raleigh, if thou hast the grace, humble thyself to the King and confess thy treasons!"

Raleigh was badly shaken. Confession upon confession cancelled out confession. The one in his pocket was merely one more confession, though he believed it the true one. The Lord Chief Justice asked if Cobham had been promised anything by the commissioners for his charges against Raleigh. The commissioners protested vigorously.

"I daresay not," Raleigh interjected, "but my Lord Cobham received a letter from his wife that there was no way to save his life but to accuse me. I pray you hear me . . . You have heard a strange tale of a strange man: you shall see how many souls this Cobham has. For me, he is a poor, silly, base, dishonourable soul." And he then brought forth his letter from Cobham and asked that it be read.

Coke flew into a final rage and utterly refused. Once more Cecil unexpectedly interrupted to ask that it be read.

Coke turned on him furiously. "My Lord Cecil, mar not a good cause!"

Cecil answered tartly, "Mr. Attorney, you must not come here to show me what to do."

Coke was forced to yield.

Cobham said that "to clear my conscience, satisfy the world with truth, and free myself from the cry of blood, I protest upon my soul and before God and his angels, I never had conference with you in any treason, nor was ever moved by you to the things I heretofore accused you of; and for anything I know, you are as innocent and as clear from any treasons against the King as is any subject living. . . . And God so deal with me and have mercy on my soul, as this true!"

Despite Raleigh's evidence, the jury took just fifteen minutes to find him guilty. The Lord Chief Justice then set the black cap on his head and spoke the terrible words of bloody execution.

11
A Game of Execution

Raleigh's trial had a profound effect upon the future of English law. Never before had English justice been so degraded. Men began to see that the law had been built for the State. It did not provide for the right of an individual man to be judged on the facts. The same Walter Raleigh who had been so ferociously attacked on his way to the trial was now a hero — no, *more* than a hero. He was a figure of immense dignity who had "behaved himself so worthily, so wisely, so temperately, that in half a day the mind of all the company was changed from the extremist hate to the greatest pity," an eyewitness wrote.

A Scotsman, Lord Hay, who had hated Raleigh out of loyalty to the King, told James that, whereas at first "he would have gone a hundred miles to have seen him hanged, he would now have gone a thousand to save his life."

Never was a man so hated and so popular within so short a time.

Back in prison, Raleigh lost his courage. He knew how horrifying was the death to which he had been sentenced — to be hanged, drawn, and quartered.

"I plainly perceive," he wrote to Bess, "that my death was determined upon from the first day." His reaction was so intense that he could hardly endure the three weeks that he must wait before death released him. "Oh, God, I cannot live to think how I am derided — the scorns, the cruel words of lawyers, the infamous taunts and despites, to be made a wonder and a spectacle! Oh, death, destroy the memory of these and lay me up in dark forgetfulness."

Then he was swept by the helplessness of his wife and son, and he suddenly determined to fight for his life. He wrote letters pleading with the King. But when they were completely ignored, he took back his pride and his bold high spirit. "Get those letters if it be possible," he later wrote Bess, "wherein I sued for my life . . . And know it, dear wife, that your son is the child of a true man who, in his own respect, despises Death and all his misshapen and ugly forms. My true wife, farewell. Bless my poor boy; pray for me. May the true God hold you both in His arms."

Lord Brooke was executed on December 6. But when his bleeding head was held up for the crowd to see, and the executioner spoke the formal words, "God save the King," no one echoed them saved the sheriff. Rumours of a reprieve began to circulate . . . rumours that Cobham would again confess to Raleigh's innocence.

The King had given no sign of mercy except to soften the terrible verdict "to be hanged, drawn, and quartered" to a beheading Bess had begged Cecil to intervene. And others, powerful at court, had pleaded for Raleigh's life.

On December 9, three more of the conspirators, including Cobham, were to be executed. For all Raleigh knew, he too might die that day. He spent the preceding night writing a letter to Bess in which he put down all his love for her and for their son. "I would not with my last will present you with sorrows, dear Bess. Let them go to the grave with me, and be buried in the dust. . . .

Bear my destruction gently, and with a heart like your-self. . . ." He also wrote a poem, and here is the first verse:

> *Give me my scallop shell of quiet,*
> *My staff of faith to walk upon,*
> *My scrip of joy, immortal diet,*
> *My bottle of salvation,*
> *My gown of glory, hope's true gauge.*
> *And thus I'll take my pilgrimage.*

The next day he had one clue that he might live a little longer. At the hour appointed for the executions, Markham, one of the conspirators, was led to the scaffold. He knelt and put his head on the block. Then followed a grisly comedy — one that showed the strange mind of the new king. Raleigh, who had been ordered to stand in the window of Wolversey Castle and watch the executions, could only stare in dumb amazement.

As the axe was about to fall, the sheriff seized the executioner's arm and then leaned over to receive a warrant from a boy struggling in the crowd. Markham stood up and was led down the steps.

Grey, another of the conspirators, eventually took his place and the same odd and cruel procedure was re-peated. Finally Cobham knelt by the executioner's block, was saved in the same melodramatic fashion, and was then joined by Markham and Grey.

Raleigh, bewildered and appalled, watched this cruel sport not knowing what it meant. He saw all three prisoners led away, the scaffold dismantled. Then he was told — the King had decided that Brooke's execution was enough. But for some reason it pleased him to extend the sufferings of the others. On the day before the executions, he had signed two sets of warrants: one stayed the execution of Cobham, Markham, and Grey; the other ordered their deaths.

A Scottish page boy, John Gibb, was the only one let in on the secret. Gibb was given the warrant which stayed the execution, and the other warrant, ordering

the deaths, was sent to the Sheriff of Hampshire. Gibb was to appear at the very last moment, when all hope had been abandoned, and save their lives.

It was a cruel and melodramatic game — and almost fatal. Gibb was caught in the crowd around the scaffold and, because he was a boy, he was thrust out of the yard with the other boys. He saw Markham kneel, and the headsman prepare his axe. He shouted with all his might, crying out the name of the sheriff and waving his warrant as high as he could.

When the sheriff seized the headsman's axe, and climbed off the scaffold to read the new warrant, he too showed a cruel sense of humour. He told Markham that he had been given a two-hour reprieve, and locked him in a hall.

Grey was then led out, and the same miserable farce played through once more with variations. Grey was told that he had an hour's grace, for Lord Cobham was to be executed ahead of him. Then when Cobham knelt to die, the sheriff intervened again and said there was still one more thing to be done. He ordered Grey and Markham brought back to the scaffold.

When at length the three men stood before him, both spectators and prisoners were shaken and hysterical. The sheriff delivered a lecture on their terrible crimes, the justice of the trials and verdicts, and the execution that awaited them. When he finally asked, "Are you penitent?" what could they murmur? "Then," said the sheriff, his voice changing like an actor's to great jollity, "see the mercy of your king who of himself has sent a countermand and given you your lives."

Cheers and applause swept over this horrible farce, and the three prisoners broke down and wept.

For some time Raleigh's fate was unsettled. Finally he was told that the King's mercy had extended to him as well. Though his sentence had not been commuted, his life had been reprieved. He would be confined to the Tower for the rest of his life.

Raleigh was now in his early fifties. A man of smaller

character would probably have considered his usefulness entirely at an end. But Raleigh had already given way to his despair; it was now behind him. He had to plan for the future, and that future must contain elements which would keep him alive both physically and spiritually. In prison he found his greatness.

Bess and Wat were his essential links to life. Within a few weeks they were allowed to live with him. The Tower was of course not a common prison. At one time it had been a palace, and the new sovereigns of England had spent the days before their coronation in the state apartments there. The rooms were, on the whole, comfortable and attractive, although very damp. In a short time, Raleigh had succeeded in getting one of the handsomest sets of rooms in the Tower, and he was allowed to keep his own servants — at his own expense, of course. The next step must be the daring and improbable one of obtaining his freedom.

However hopeless this might seem, he had to believe and to act as though it were possible. He kept up a running fire of appeals to the King, the Privy Council, and Cecil. And he demanded the utmost respect to be shown him in prison. This was very important.

One of his most urgent problems was his total loss of funds. James had stripped him of his offices. In addition, everything accumulated for twenty years had been swept away, save Sherborne. The Howard family had been granted Raleigh's wine patent, and they now demanded and seized all the arrears which Raleigh had not collected and which by law belonged to him. Like ghouls, the commissioners descended on his beloved estate at Sherborne. They sold his cattle and began to claim the furnishings in the house.

Bess went in tears to Cecil to ask for compassion and justice. The arrears — and Sherborne — were all she and Raleigh had in the world.

What were Cecil's feelings — he who had so carefully

planned Raleigh's downfall? Three times he had spoken
for him at his trial, and he had wept when the verdict
came in.

Now he intervened with the Howards and called off
the despoilers of the estate. He also undertook to have
ratified a deed in which Raleigh, several years before,
had given the estate to his son. Cecil saw that trustees
were appointed to protect Bess and Wat. He wrote
Raleigh several unsigned letters of cautious encourage-
ment. Bess and Raleigh's gratitude could scarcely be
measured.

But now a new fear came. Someone in the Tower died
of the plague.

The plague was the most dreaded disease of the day,
and Raleigh hurriedly sent Bess and Wat outside the
infested walls. He himself had to take his chances. Bess
rented a house within sight of the Tower, and during the
winter she gave birth to a second son, whom they named
Carew.

The warden of the Tower was still Sir George Harvey.
He was the man who had, before Raleigh's trial, injured
him by witholding vital evidence. His son had been
Raleigh's friend. Now, watching Raleigh, and seeing his
resolute determination to keep both mind and body alive,
Harvey also became the prisoner's friend. They walked
on the walls of the Tower and talked of many things.

Since botany interested Raleigh, Harvey gave him a
plot of earth where he could grow and study plants.
Since chemistry intrigued him, Harvey allowed Raleigh
to build a small furnace where he could assay ores. He
also permitted him a tiny laboratory for chemical
research.

So Raleigh spent his first bitterly cold winter and
spring. His chemical experiments were so skilful that
he mastered the art of making fresh water out of salt—
a kind of alchemy greatly desired in that day of long
sea voyages. But Raleigh never disclosed the secret, and
it died with him. He also distilled a "great cordial"

D

made of animal, vegetable, and mineral elements which, for over a century, was used by doctors.

The Tower had a famous exhibit of wild animals — one of the sights of London. But the sight of Raleigh, walking on the Tower walls, became almost as popular as a glimpse of the wild beasts. Boatloads of admirers drifted by, calling to him and waving.

Distinguished visitors to the Tower were equally charmed by the sight of him working in his garden plot, and they stopped to chat and bring him word from the larger world outside.

Raleigh saw, from the walls of the Tower, not only his supporters but also the rich and varied life of the river and the far horizon. It is not hard to imagine how often he must have stood motionless and followed with his eyes the seagoing ships as they left London Pool for their long voyages. His dreams of land claimed for England, of riches brought from the New World, never left him. Guiana obsessed him as a possible means of his release. It seemed incredible that a man like James — always poor, always greedy for money — would not see how great a treasure lay in Guiana

The first two years of imprisonment were comparatively happy. The time was filled with the activities which pleased his mind, the tender companionship of Bess, and the baby Carew, and the hours he spent every day teaching Wat.

Wat was a vivid, extremely intelligent boy, gay and gifted. He adored his father, and yet was no meek and mild facsimile. They argued like friends. Although Raleigh often chaffed at Wat's stubborn determination to find out things for himself he never chastised him in the harsh way of Elizabethan fathers.

At the end of two years, Harvey was replaced as warden by Sir William Waad, who had been one of the commissioners at Raleigh's trial. A small and mean-spirited man, Waad let it be known that he was the fount of all authority. But Bess had her own ways of defying

authority. Always pleasant and courteous, but always
determined, she drove in her coach straight into the
Tower courtyard. This was against regulations and left
Waad in a fury. He retaliated by introducing new regulations. When the bell of the Tower rang in the late after-
noon, prisoners must go to their cells and stay there for
the night. Wives must leave. Wives were not to drive into
the prison in their coaches.

He then fixed his attention on Raleigh's garden. It
was producing sinister plants, he reported to Cecil,
and this indicated some large conspiracy.

The Gunpowder Plot had recently frightened James
out of his wits. This plot — to blow up King, Lords, and
Commons assembled for the opening of Parliament —
had been discovered only hours before the appointed
time.

The wide dragnet of inquiry set in motion by the plot
reached into the Tower, and Raleigh was taken for
questioning to the House of Lords. This was Waad's
opportunity for further persecutions. During his prisoner's
absence, he built a brick wall that would confine Raleigh
to a narrow plot where he would have no view of the
world or the world of him.

This was the kind of thing that amused rather than
angered Raleigh. He loved to make petty men seem even
smaller. Climbing out on top of the wall, he walked with
an even better view of the world — higher before the
eyes of the people.

As his fame became almost legendary, his enemies
became more vicious. This was perhaps natural, for some
of them — like the King — must have known how wrongly
they had used him. And the fact that Raleigh's friends
were reaching into higher and higher places must have
made the King's hatred even greater.

James's wife, Queen Anne, who was a sister of the
King of Denmark, became Raleigh's friend and great
admirer. She was a frivolous and foolish woman with a
good-natured contempt for her husband and a deep and

genuine admiration for Raleigh. She firmly believed that his "great cordial" had cured her during an illness.

When her brother came on a state visit to England, the Queen asked him to put in a word for Raleigh. Her brother did not need any promptings. As the king of a seagoing country, he greatly admired Raleigh, the sailor, and wanted him as Admiral of his fleet. He asked his brother-in-law to pardon Raleigh, but James pretended not to hear.

Young men of beauty and grace appealed very much to King James. One of his favourites was Robert Carr a Scotsman like himself. Carr was a weak and foolish young man but very handsome. First James knighted him, and then he made him Earl of Somerset.

This led to a new suffering for Raleigh. To be an earl required money and estates, for such a title carried many obligations. One day Cecil, who had originally interceded to protect Raleigh's estate at Sherborne, suggested that the King take Sherborne for Carr.

Cecil well knew, as did James, that through a clerk's error the deed of conveyance which protected Sherborne was a faulty one. Nothing could be done about it, once the error had been made. But Cecil had reassured both Raleigh and Bess that the mistake would not be held against their rightful claims. Now the King, through the Court of Exchequer, called upon Raleigh to show a proper title to the estate. All Raleigh had to show was the flawed conveyance. The judgment was found in the King's favour.

Raleigh could scarcely have felt much surprise knowing all that he did of betrayals, but to Bess this was one blow too much. She had kept up her courage and spirit, fought her husband's enemies, raised her sons, and always continued to have hope. But at this unexpected and devasting blow she fell into hysterics. For the first time in her life she cast blame at her husband.

Raleigh was utterly distraught by her reproaches.

He wrote painfully to Cecil—not knowing of Cecil's duplicity—begging as he had never begged before. He even wrote a letter to Carr, imploring him not to take advantage of a clerk's error "to give me and mine our last fatal blow, by obtaining from His Majesty the inheritance of my children lost in law for want of words."

Bess even fell on her knees before the King, begging God Almighty to punish those who had so wrongfully exposed her and her poor children to ruin and beggary.

But the King would not look at her, muttering only, "I mun have the land, I mun have it for Carr."

Hope was quite stamped out. Not only was Raleigh forced to see his wife and two sons brought to the edge of poverty, but he was obliged to face the fact that Cecil was his enemy.

Now Raleigh was stripped of all illusions. All he had left were those dearest to him. But in that dauntless mind of his, an affirmation of hope and life was beginning to take shape.

12

A Tragic Blow

Shortly after Raleigh's imprisonment, Queen Anne had begun to visit the Tower on one pretext or another. While there she always found a reason to speak with Raleigh, and often she had her older son, Prince Henry, with her. Presently the Prince began to come alone.

Henry was thirteen years old — the same age as Wat Raleigh. He was a keen, handsome, intelligent boy, and Londoners adored him. King Hal the Ninth, they called him, and ambassadors wrote home careful accounts of this ideal Prince of Wales.

It is not surprising that Henry grew to idealise Raleigh. Raleigh was the complete opposite of James, and Henry both distrusted and disliked his father. Raleigh knew all the things that Henry wished to know; their dreams and interests were the same. Henry turned to Raleigh for advice on the most private matters — even, in time, on the nationality and type of princess he should marry. This was taking Raleigh into affairs of the highest state

Raleigh must have had a remarkable attitude toward boys — remarkable certainly in an age when children were treated with great severity and often brutality. Not only did his own son love him passionately, but Will

Cecil also loved him more dearly than his own father. To all three of these boys Raleigh gave his love, his courtesy, and his deep attention.

"Only my father," said Henry, "would keep such a bird in a cage."

Raleigh probably knew that his friendship with the Prince did him great harm in the King's eyes. But in his own eyes it was like a rising sun.

Henry loved all things to do with water and, not least, ships and tales of far-off places. Who could supply the tales better than Raleigh? . . . Tales of Guiana and Virginia and the vast Atlantic.

Plans were afoot to make Virginia into a permanent colony, and Henry talked eagerly to those men who came to the Tower to consult with Raleigh.

Although Raleigh's conviction for treason had cancelled his patent rights in Virginia, the new plans were all based on his experience and on the information he had been gathering for many years. Many who had worked with him in the past were now reviving the old schemes. Within three years, four separate groups began to think and plan. They talked with Raleigh; they drew on his dreams and his practical knowledge; they stirred him anew.

But Virginia had never held Raleigh's thoughts and dreams as had Guiana. With every new move toward Virginia, he added a plea that he might be set free to explore Guiana for the King. All through the years — even these years in the Tower — he had managed through friends to send a ship at regular intervals to Guiana "to comfort and assure the people that they despair not."

One of the most unusual sights in the Tower — or in London, for that matter — was the Guianan chief who for two years voluntarily shared Raleigh's imprisonment, and walked on the walls with him.

But the Spaniards still had their fort and garrisons along the Orinoco, and peace with the Spaniards was still more important to James than gold.

All this the Prince knew, for all that Raleigh heard, planned, and discussed was shared with his future king. At Henry's urging, Raleigh wrote a letter to Queen Anne, begging for a chance to "reap honour and commodity" from Guiana for the King. But the King paid no attention to his wife. His only emotion was a deeper anger at Raleigh for enlisting the support of his family.

Yet in the early spring of 1607, James authorised three small ships to sail across the Atlantic and try again where Raleigh's previous colony had failed. He did it partly to please his son.

Raleigh watched the preparations from the Tower, and he was one of the first to be told when word came back that Jamestown had been settled in that same region to which he had directed the first colonists more than twenty years before

The Spanish ambassador in London, writing in some nervousness to his king, said that Raleigh's advice and recommendations were fully followed by the Council of Virginia. "The Old Pirate" might be locked up, but what good was that if his power was still great enough to reach through prison bars?

Raleigh tried to work through Cecil, who was now Earl of Salisbury. He told Cecil that a rock from Guiana had been brought to him and analysed, showing an impressive amount of gold. He knew where the mine was, and the gold was so close to the surface it could be scooped up. Raleigh sang one steady tune: gold, gold, gold, for a greedy king and greedy courtiers.

At last in 1609 the Prince, who was now fifteen years old, got permission for Robert Harcourt to take an expedition to Guiana. Harcourt was familiar with Raleigh's thoughts and plans. He was a follower of Raleigh's philosophy of friendship and self-government for the Indians.

In May, 1609, Harcourt arrived in Guiana with sixty men, and made a formal claim to the land around Wiapoco. Gathering a group of chiefs together, he told them that he came in the name of their friend Raleigh, who thought of them with great concern, and had sent him to defend them against their enemies.

All along the coast, Harcourt found that Raleigh's name was a living thing — even fourteen years after his visit.

For three years at least, Harcourt's brother Michael maintained a trading post on the land he had claimed. He even built a small factory to make hatchets, knives, beads, and mirrors (all greatly wanted by the Indians). These were exchanged for sugar cane, cotton, flax, tobacco, hardwoods, and dyestuffs.

To the future king of England, these discussions and expeditions were an education in statecraft. A great navy was a part of his concept of expanding English power. Raleigh and he talked tirelessly of the kinds of ships a modern navy would need. Raleigh made a model of a new design and, with the Prince as intermediary, worked with Phineas Pett, master builder of the navy, on several notable ships.

The man whom James had humiliated and put away in the Tower had won from James his dearest treasure, his elder son. James could do nothing about it, for he was a little afraid of this son, but Raleigh's influence over the Prince became one more act of treason.

The King was kept informed by Sir William Waad, the Lieutenant of the Tower, of all Henry's visits to Raleigh. What James could never know was the innocence and lack of treason in all this. Raleigh loved the giving and receiving of knowledge more than anything in the world. In that strange disinterested way of his — which had got him into so much trouble — he could no more fail in candour than he could fail in breath. He thought about the Prince's questions and his own answers, and began to write for the Prince's instruction a remarkable book, *A History of the World, Beginning with the Creation.* It became his great monument.

His intention was not to retell history in a conventional way. He believed that men's lives — and therefore history — were the outcome of moral attitudes. He believed that what happened in history was the result of thought and behaviour. He believed that historical consequences were never capricious, always just.

Although the scope of the book was vast, its pattern was intimate and dramatic. He swept together past and present. He would pause in the description of a Persian battle to recall an adventure of his own in France.

There is something wonderfully attractive about this man, legally dead, economically ruined, shut off from the world, yet cheerfully performing an intellectual feat before which most free men would hesitate.

The King's anger and frustration grew. He complained

that there was no control over "the lawless liberty of the Tower, so long fostered with hopes exorbitant." The "hopes exorbitant" were largely fostered by the Prince, who had a way of overawing his father.

Henry had said often and publicly that Raleigh's trial had been a cruel violation of a man's rights. He had studied the full record of the trial. He was candidly and patiently waiting for the day he came of age to obtain Raleigh's release.

Since Raleigh's death sentence had never been lifted, he was technically dead in law. Henry intended that Raleigh should not only be delivered from prison, but should also have full restoration of property and a full statement of innocence, so that the law should be forced to acknowledge that he lived. In public, he had drawn from the King that "Raleigh should be delivered out of the Tower before Christmas of 1612."

Henry took another step. Outraged when he heard that Sherborne had been given to Robert Carr, he "came," according to Carew Raleigh, "with some anger to his father . . . and in such language that sounded rather like a demand than an entreaty, claimed Sherborne for himself."

The remarkable thing is that he got his way. The King was forced to buy back Sherborne from Carr and give it to his son.

Some of the King's nobles followed Henry's example and consulted Raleigh in the Tower on matters of state. What should they do about James's plans to join Catholic and Protestant Europe to Great Britain? (This was the new name given to the union of England, Scotland, and Wales.) . . . And Henry asked: What did Raleigh think of the proposed marriage between himself and the Infanta of Spain, and what about the plan to marry Henry's sister Elizabeth to the son of the Roman Catholic Duke of Savoy?

Raleigh thought poorly of both proposals. Henry commanded him to write down his reasons for opposing both plans so that he and all the world could understand.

This was very bold indeed. But Raleigh was still as indifferent to consequences as ever. He wrote two *Discourses* against these marriages, and they were startlingly effective statements of foreign policy. Of course it was an insane situation: a prisoner in the Tower, still under sentence of death, writing as though he were a master of England.

His moral strength lay perhaps in his absolute assumption that England was a great power. Even England's kings did not always believe this. But to Raleigh there was no doubt, and never had been. He would oppose with all his might any plan which tried to reduce England to an inferior position — as Spain had spent a hundred years attempting to do.

Raleigh's *Discourses* were intolerable to James. The double marriage had been the basis of his dream of peace in Europe and security for Great Britain. Prince Henry now refused to consider a marriage with a princess of Spain, and he persuaded his sister to refuse the son of the Duke of Savoy.

Cecil shared the King's anger. Here like a ghost was the old Raleigh rising again. But the time had passed when they could put Raleigh to sudden death. They must wait.

Then Cecil died suddenly, early in the year 1612. He was worn out, having served faithfully two of his rulers.

When Robert Carr, the young favourite of the King, snatched up Cecil's position as First Secretary, Raleigh and Bess were quick to realise that this inexperienced, vain, and foolish man might be susceptible to some of the Raleigh magic. It was a faint hope, for Carr was a closer friend even than James of the Spanish ambassador. But Raleigh was too shrewd to underestimate his own power.

The year of 1612 seemed the year of hope. Cecil's enmity had been buried with him, and the Prince would come of age. Then fell the blow which rocked Raleigh to his soul, and perhaps changed the course of English history.

At the wedding of the Princess Elizabeth to a German prince, Prince Henry was burning with fever. The next day he seemed better and went riding with his new brother-in-law, but at dinner that night he fainted.

The doctors put him to bed and diagnosed his illness as best they could. The wedding festivities had to go on because otherwise too many people would be disappointed and too much money lost.

Henry's mother, the Queen, was in despair. She firmly believed that the famous elixir which Raleigh made in his laboratory at the Tower would save her son's life, as it had saved her life many years before. But the King refused permission to administer it.

When the fever continued, the Queen pleaded with the King to send for Raleigh's elixir. At length James agreed. A courtier secured the compound from Raleigh, and started back to the palace without delay. Raleigh said all would be well if it were administered immediately.

But they had all reckoned without the King. Before the courtier could return from the Tower, James went hunting. He did not come back for several days. Without the King's permission no one dared administer the elixir obtained from Raleigh.

When it was at last given, the fever broke. Henry's eyes grew clear, and he spoke. But he was too weak to survive. Within a few hours he died.

The Queen promptly charged that he had been poisoned, and she pointed her finger at Robert Carr.

13
Return to Life

Raleigh's grief at the death of Henry was a double grief—
the grief of a man for a son and of a subject for a wise
prince, made wise by the qualities Raleigh had helped
to shape. It was a blow so cruel one could hardly measure
its consequences.

Raleigh closed his *History of the World*. He had
brought it to the year 132 B.C. Its last words were his
farewell to Henry. "My lyre is changed into the sound
of mourning, and my song into the voices of people
weeping."

With Henry's death went Raleigh's chance of freedom
"before Christmas." And James sold Sherborne back to
Carr at a neat profit.

Perhaps Henry had been poisoned, or perhaps he had
died of typhoid fever. (Raleigh's elixir is now believed
to have contained quinine, which he had learned about in
Guiana.) Whatever the truth, Robert Carr was soon
involved in a scandal that made the Queen's fears seem
only too reasonable. The scandal also affected Raleigh's
future.

Carr had fallen in love with Frances Howard, who was
married to the third Earl of Essex. Divorces were almost

impossible to get in those days, but through trickery and deceit the church was eventually persuaded to permit divorce proceedings to begin. Everything was going smoothly until a former friend of Carr, named Overbury, threatened to expose all Carr's lies and all Frances' intrigues.

Overbury was arrested on a minor charge and put in the Tower with promises of quick freedom. Very quick indeed — he died in terrible agony showing all the symptoms of poison.

Rumours flew about. Had Overbury paid the price of refusing to help Carr in further crime? Was it Overbury, perhaps, who had administered poison to Henry and was he threatening to speak?

Carr and Frances were married as quickly as possible.

Carr, as First Secretary, lasted only a very short time. James had to acknowledge that Carr was not very gifted and was badly tainted with scandal. He gave the position to Sir Ralph Winwood.

How Raleigh must have smiled. How his hope was at last justified! For Ralph Winwood was an old friend and admirer, and a frequent visitor to Raleigh in the Tower. They saw eye to eye on matters of policy. Now they could begin to plan in ways close to Raleigh's heart.

Slowly the scandal which Carr and his wife had generated began to gather momentum. First a woman, humble and ordinary, was accused of stealing a ring from Frances. The woman said the ring belonged to her, because Frances had never paid her for a slow poison prepared for Frances' first husband, the Earl of Essex. Frances immediately withdrew her charge of theft.

Now, like vermin coming out of the cracks, all those who had assisted in Frances' criminal deeds began to appear. Sir Ralph Winwood, a calm, shrewd man, took control. Distrusting the whole crew, he ordered the new Lieutenant of the Tower, Sir Gervase Elwes, to answer

certain questions. Sir Gervase confessed that he had received his appointment as Lieutenant in order to supervise the poisoning of Overbury. And he had received it from Lord Henry Howard, Frances' uncle — and also Raleigh's most ruthless enemy.

Even James could no longer try to conceal the depths of the scandal. The trial of the Carrs was ordered. Coke was now Lord Chief Justice, and James expected that Coke would do his bidding and completely exonerate the Carrs.

But Coke surprised and dismayed him. The trial became such an appalling disclosure of guilt that even the King's frantic efforts could not prevent a verdict of guilty against the Carrs.

The King, however, used his Prerogative and saved them from execution. They were sent to the Tower. Frances, lodged in the apartment where Overbury had died, fell into such hysterical screams that another room had to be found for her. The only other suitable apartment was Raleigh's.

For some time Raleigh's release had been in the air. Because the King's desperate need for money was an open secret, Windwood had urged Raleigh to write letters glittering with talk of gold. Raleigh had done so, begging for a chance to "die for the King, and not by the King."

A little judicious bribery of courtiers close to the King had, also, a quickening effect. Frances Carr's screams supplied the finishing touch.

In March, 1616, the Lieutenant of the Tower received the warrant releasing Raleigh — for the express purpose of preparing a voyage to Guiana. After thirteen long years the gates clanged open and Raleigh — a man legally dead — emerged into the world.

There was Bess waiting in her coach. He got in somewhat stiffly, for the long years of the damp Tower had made his old Cadiz wound painful. Her faithfulness, and his, which had unfailingly believed that this moment would come, deepened their greeting. Their love had been unwavering.

The coach crossed the drawbridge, circled Tower Hill, and drove into the world he had never left in his thoughts.

14
Return to Guiana

This man who came back into the world was no longer a young man. He was ill and grey. He knew that the King's good will was not be trusted, and he knew in his heart that he was too old for Guiana. But being Raleigh he found his old zest, his old faith that England's future lay in a vast and strong empire around the world.

Setting out to see London, he found a greatly changed city, with thousands of new people. This tall, handsome, grey-haired man must have drawn many glances and probably some recognition as he stood in The Strand looking at his old home, Durham House.

London had become a sprawling city clamorous with coaches which took up most of the narrow streets, a London of new buildings and awful squalor, of new conduits and water mains and the old piles of offal in the streets. New fashions were decking the men and women, but the same old street cries delighted his ear.

Although Raleigh was forbidden the Court, he went nonetheless. The former banqueting hall, where many times he had dined with his great queen, had been pulled down and a new one put up in its place.

He saw his old friends, including the playwright,

Ben Johnson, who had been Wat's tutor and had taken him to France.

Wat was now in Holland. Raleigh promptly sent for him. Wat would go with him to Guiana.

What Wat most wanted! What Bess most dreaded.

Raleigh returned to the Tower to fetch away his books and papers. Entering his old apartment in the Bloody Tower, he came face to face with Carr, the man who had taken Sherborne and harried him with cruelties both large and small. The spoke with a fusillade of words. The meeting was too emotional for either man to remain calm.

Raleigh had been released as a pawn in a game the King was playing — not the kind of bold game Elizabeth had played, but a niggardly game full of political tricks. Raleigh had to make his moves with the greatest of care. He was aware of his helplessness. He was aware that if the marriage of the King's second son, Charles, to a Spanish princess — up one day, down the next — was successfully concluded, he would be sacrified to Spain.

The most sinister, overshadowing figure in London was Count Gondomar, the Spanish ambassador. Gondomar had responded with quick alarm to the release of "Sir Vate Rauli — the dreaded Gualtero" from prison. He wrote urgent letters to his own king, saying the Spanish navy must be strengthened now that this tired, grey man was out of prison. He begged that no Spanish ships set forth without a convoy. He even returned to Spain to make his king grasp the full implications of danger from "Spain's terrible scourge."

Gondomar was an extraordinary man. Unlike many diplomatic Spaniards who were very dignified, he had become a rollicking figure at James's court. He had once written to his own king saying that it was no problem to manage the King of England. He had only to pretend to be his admiring pupil no matter what he thought of him in reality. At the same time, Gondomar was very clever at anticipating James's money needs, and would slip him a sizable amount in gold on one pretext or another. The King was almost as charmed by this tall, slender, balding, cold-eyed man as he was by his young favourites.

Gondomar had used his power to try to prevent the release of Raleigh. And Raleigh and his friends were well aware of Gondomar's intrigues and the long shadow he cast. But mostly they had to work in the dark for when it came to the subject of Spain and Raleigh, even Winwood, the First Secretary, was misled and refused information by James.

Some element of risk might have been cancelled had Raleigh been willing to listen to the flattering proposals of the French and Savoyard ambassadors. They offered him large sums of money to sail under their own countries' flags. But Raleigh was possessed by a dream: that England must have Guiana and give it "good government."

As Raleigh worked feverishly to complete the building, provisioning, and manning of his seven ships, the King and Gondomar walked in the gardens and halls of the palace. Gondomar threatened and bullied. He told James that the King of Spain was a in a rage. He forced the King of England to tell him all "the pirate's" plans and obtain for him Raleigh's secret list of ships, arms, and ports of call.

Raleigh tried his best to withhold this list from the King, and he did not give it up until James solemnly promised, "on the word and hand of a King," to reveal the information to *no one*. The list was in Gondomar's hand within a few minutes. Exact copies were sent promptly to Spain.

While Winwood shrewdly used his power as First Secretary to find out what the King was concealing from him, James drew up Raleigh's commission as Admiral. He struck out the traditional words, "Our trusty and well beloved." In their place he put Raleigh "under peril of the law" if he challenged in any way Spain's claim to Guiana. At the same time James recognized England's rights to the lands claimed more than twenty years before.

"Under peril of the law" — what did it mean?

It meant if the expedition failed Raleigh could be put to death.

But how could it succeed with Spain in full knowledge of all his plans?

It seemed as though everyone in London knew that Raleigh was sailing into a trap. At the last moment, the French ambassador came aboard Raleigh's flag-ship, the *Destiny,* to inspect the modern equipment and latest design, and offer him once again the protection of France.

This time, Raleigh did not reject it outright. He left an escape hatch. When he returned from Guiana, he would again talk with the ambassador. For he was determined to come back. He had become more and more concerned, however, that his sentence of execution — laid upon him fourteen years before — had never been lifted. How could he dare leave without a practical assurance that he would not be done to death if he returned? Friends suggested bribery.

In a final effort to settle the question of a pardon, he turned to an old friend for advice. He and Francis Bacon, now Lord Keeper of the Great Seal and Lord Chancellor, "continued walking" as Bacon put it, "in Grey's Inn walks a long while." Raleigh wondered if the King might not prove susceptible if a large enough sum of cash were offered.

Bacon said, "Money is the knee-timber of your voyage, do not use up funds. Upon my life, your commission as Admiral is as good a pardon for all former offences as the law of England can afford you."

What Bess felt about all this can be imagined. In some ways this voyage was even harder for her than his imprisonment. The dangers were as great; the outcome weighted with equal uncertainty — and they would be separated. In addition, she would be parted from her elder son. He had been old enough to know her many anguishes; she had often had to be mother and father to him. Wat's wild ways she had fondly seen as a reliving of his father's youth. She knew that neither Wat nor Raleigh would listen to any pleas from her. Wat was wild to go, and Raleigh believed it was a way to tame him.

The relationship of Wat and his father was filled with high temperament on both sides. Some of Raleigh's friends asked if Wat could be trusted to keep out of trouble. Raleigh did not need trouble, but he desperately needed those he could trust — whether a son, a nephew, or an old and trusted friend like Lawrence Keymis.

He had a crew which dismayed him, but what kind men would volunteer to serve under a commander who could be hanged for either failure or success? They had to be men who either prized his genius or were leaving "their country for their country's good."

Raleigh tried to make the best of them, putting responsibility on a few. As a good commander, he attempted to weld the whole into a self-respecting and disciplined crew. His Orders to the Fleet were not only good orders but showed respect for his men by giving his reasons for prohibiting "smoking between decks," blasphemy, mistreatment of women and Indians.

In June, 1617, he went down to Devon to take possession of his ships. Devon treated Bess and him as though they were king and queen. They were feasted from one end of the county to the other. Yet Bess had to pledge her jewels before provisions would be taken aboard ship. And at the last moment, Raleigh had to raise several hundred more pounds to meet a cash-on-delivery demand. He had already gone to every possible source to raise the immense amount of money required for the voyage.

The fleet, sailing out of Plymouth Harbour, brought tears to many eyes. It was so gallant, so reminiscent of the glorious days of the past. In grandness and beauty, the swelling sails moved like great birds. But some of the old calamities came to life again. The Channel storms were the worst since the summer of the Great Armada, nearly thirty years before.

Three times Raleigh was driven back to port. After the third effort, he put into Ireland for repairs. When at length he sailed into the Atlantic, James notified Gondomar.

The Spanish government promptly sent word to every Spanish port "to put an end to this enterprise as well as to the lives of those who sail with Don Gualtero Rauli."

But even this did not content Gondomar. He wrote to his king that Raleigh should be pursued by the Spanish fleet and hanged in the square of Seville. He could speak with more than usual candour, for one of the British Privy Councillors had written a letter to Gondomar in which he had said, "His Majesty is very disposed and determined against Raleigh, and will join the King of Spain in ruining him, but he wishes this resolution to be kept secret for some little while, in order that, in the interim, he may keep an eye on the disposition of some of the people here."

An epidemic was raging among Raleigh's men, and tempestuous seas had already drowned one ship and its crew. The storms were followed by a hellish calm in which the weak and helpless were trapped under a blazing sun. Each day more bodies were buried in the sea. October was the worst of all. Raleigh himself became ill, and for nearly a month was too weak to move. Men who had left England as the scum and scrapings of a crew became heroes. Skeletons manned the ships. When at last they dropped anchor in the muddy bottom of the Cayenne River in Guiana, Raleigh stood weakly in the bow looking at this brave new world which he had held in his mind for so long.

"Sweet Heart," he wrote to Bess that very day, ". . . God that gave me a strong heart in all my adversities hath also now strengthened it in the hell-fire of heat.

(We will succeed) if the diligent care at London to make our strength known to the Spanish king have not taught him to fortify all the entrances against us. Howsoever, we must make the adventure. . . ." Though some irreplaceable men had died—his general, his surgeon, his master refiner, his provost marshal—Wat was in blooming health; and he, Raleigh, might "be King of the Indians (for) my name hath still lived among them."

One of the first to greet him was the chief who had shared two years of his imprisonment in the Tower and had walked on the walls to the delight and wonder of

London. With what affection they greeted each other! He came in his jewels and his parrot feathers, and ordered Raleigh carried off the pest-ridden ship into a tent. There he was fed lemon juice and pineapples.

Wat was bursting for action. He had survived all the catastrophes. He could not get enough of this world which had existed in his imagination since childhood. The Indian chiefs, honouring his father in their cere-monial clothes, moved him as deeply as they moved Raleigh. With mounting rage, Wat heard of the cruelties they had suffered through the years from the Spanish, cruelties and tortures that were increasing in violence. Why delay? Why not go on?

Raleigh himself was in no condition to make the journey up the Orinoco. He still could not walk without help. With his best officers at the bottom of the sea, he had to give the general command to his old friend Keymis. Keymis knew the terrain, but he was neither a young man nor a captain. He was much better able to take orders than to make decisions.

Wat, volatile and inexperienced, was made captain, and Sir Walter's nephew, George Raleigh, was appointed second in command. The party set out early in December with a month's supply of provisions and Raleigh's careful instructions burned on their minds. . . . They must make their way westward to the mountain Aio "from whence you have no less than three miles to the mine . . . make trial of what depth and breadth the mine holds and whether or not it answers our hopes." Under no circum-stance were they to approach the village of San Thomé until they had explored the mine.

He stressed again and again that they were to be restrained at all costs from picking a fight with the Spaniards, "for I would not, for all the world, receive a blow from the Spaniards to the dishonour of our nation." Such a blow could not be returned under pain of Raleigh's death. He, for his part, would guard the mouth of the river so the Spaniards could not seal it up.

He watched them start up that beautiful river which he travelled in his imagination. He hoped desperately for their success, but life had taught him to expect nothing and be glad of small blessings. He himself turned with his ships toward the southwest coast of Trinidad, cruising up and down, maintaining an unbroken watch for the Spanish fleet. His little crew of convalescent men — for the strong ones had all gone with Keymis and Wat up the Orinoco — made friendly overtures of trade to the Spaniards along the coast.

The Spaniards replied with gunfire and killed two of the small number. Raleigh did not return the fire.

To relieve the tension of waiting — waiting for the Spaniards to attack, waiting for word from his men — he turned again to reflective study. He found new medicinal plants and observed the insects and enormous butterflies. He charted the strange currents. Every wandering Indian he questioned as though his life depended on it.

Then one day from a canoe load of Indians, he heard a rumour: two English captains had been killed up the Orinoco while storming a Spanish fort.

A chill cramped his heart.

15
The End of Hope

Raleigh kept a journal during these weeks of awful waiting. It was the journal of a man's soul — a man whose capacities for feeling and for insight were almost immeasurable.

He made his last entry on a day in February, 1618, when a letter from Keymis reached him. Keymis wrote that Wat had been killed.

Despite Raleigh's strict orders, Keymis had sailed on to San Thomé before locating the mine. He had put most of his men ashore just below the town, and there they had set up camp for the night. At one o'clock in the morning, the Spaniards had suddenly opened up a surprise attack from the surrounding woods. The English, wakened from their sleep, were in a wild state of confusion, but Wat Raleigh finally brought order out of chaos. "Almost before themselves knew of it" the English had pushed the attackers back as far as the town. There they found the Spanish governor with a force of regulars drawn up in battle formation. The English momentarily halted, for they were in no state or numbers to meet such an enemy — and Raleigh's instructions were burned on their minds.

But Wat would have none of that. Crying, "Come on, my hearts!" he had hurled himself at the Spanish line. Although he fell almost immediately, the victim of a dozen lance wounds, he continued to cry, "Go on! The Lord have mercy upon me, and prosper your enterprise!" His handful of men, enraged by his death, had then thrust on as though they were a thousand. Their wild charge had driven the Spanish garrison straight out of the town. On each side, five men had been lost—all of them officers.

Raleigh, reading the letter, knew that Keymis' despair was almost as deep as his own. English had killed Spanish. What hope was there now? Wat had been killed; Raleigh's life stood in forfeit.

Keymis had not yet been able to reach the mine, an achievement which might have justified all their efforts. The Spaniards were on the islands in the river and in the jungle. Although Keymis held the town, he was trapped within it. He had disobeyed all Raleigh's instructions, though he might plead that he had had no choice. (Later he insisted that the site of San Thomé had been moved since the time of the previous expedition.)

Among the Spanish records Keymis had discovered the inventory which Raleigh had prepared for King James. And he had also found copies of the expedition plans in every detail. The dates on the copies showed that even as Raleigh was sailing out of the Thames, King James had doomed him.

Eventually Keymis set off up the river with George Raleigh breaking through the Spanish blockade. They wandered indecisively, afraid to venture into the wilderness. George Raleigh, although willing and brave, knew nothing of this country. He was afraid to go alone into the jungle without provisions or a guide.

The expedition was a disaster. Keymis returned to sack San Thomé and burn it to the ground. He then ordered those of his men still alive on to their ships.

Indians came in their canoes to implore greater patience. "Do not desert us," they begged. "Gold is within a two hours' march."

But why should they listen to such old lures and perish? The survivors of the expeditionary force — 150 out of 400 men — turned desperately away, sailing back downstream. They reached the fleet on March 2.

Keymis found Raleigh a broken man. At first Sir Walter spoke gently. Then he asked a deadly question,

and he asked it as persistently as an awl boring. "Why did you not follow my last instructions?"

Keymis tried to explain; he was by no means wholly to blame. Events and a faulty memory of places known long ago had misled both Raleigh and him.

Raleigh, who had never spoken harshly to a subordinate, upbraided this old and trusted friend as though he were the devil. Raleigh was burning with fever again, but Keymis was burning with his own remorse.

Keymis tried to redeem something out of the failure. He wrote a long letter to the Earl of Arundel, one of Raleigh's powerful friends, setting things in what he claimed was their true light. Raleigh would not even look at the letter. He cried again for his dead son and his ruined hopes. He laid the blame on Keymis.

"Is this your final word?" asked Keymis, who had served Raleigh since they were young men.

Raleigh said it was. Keymis replied, "I know then, sir, what course to take."

He went into his cabin, and presently a shot was heard. A sailor calling through the locked door heard Keymis say he had discharged his pistol accidentally. But when they broke open the door, they found him dead.

His bullet had not killed him. He had finished himself with a knife stab.

Raleigh made one last desperate effort. Papers seized from the Spaniards indicated gold-workings near by. He might yet fulfil his golden hopes. But his men refused to go in search of the place. They would not stir a step. Shocked and bewildered, he was forced to give orders to sail, leaving his dear son beneath the high altar of a strange church in a foreign land.

When they reached the Leeward Islands, the fleet began to break up. One ship deserted to engage in piracy. One went home loaded with sick men. Others slipped away. Raleigh tried to hold them with wild plans of provisioning themselves along the northern coasts and then returning to seize the Spanish fleet and take it into a French port. But his men had had enough.

Raleigh's love for Bess was strong enough to give him courage to write her a remarkable letter. "I know not how to comfort you; and God knows I never knew what sorrow meant till now. . . . Comfort your heart, dearest Bess, I shall sorrow for us both. I shall sorrow the less for I have not long to sorrow, because not long to live. . . . There was never a poor man so exposed to slaughter as I was; commanded, upon my allegiance to my King, to set down not only the country but the very river by which I would enter it; to name my ship, number my men, and my artillery, and all this, sworn on the hand and word of a king to keep secret, had at once been handed to the Spanish ambassador. . . . My brains are broken, and it is a torment for me to write. The Lord bless and comfort you that you may bear patiently the death of your valiant son.

"I protest before the majesty of God that as Sir Francis Drake and Sir John Hawkins died broken-hearted when they failed of their enterprise, I could willingly do the like, did I not contend against sorrow for your sake, in hope to provide somewhat for you; and to comfort and relieve you. If I live to return, resolve yourself that it is the care for you that hath strengthened my heart."

He determined to take the only prize they had — tobacco seized in San Thomé — and trade it in Newfoundland for provisions. Then he would wander like the Flying Dutchman until he had seized gold to buy his king's favour.

Into the frozen world of Newfoundland he endeavoured to drive his weakened ship. But his crew mutinied and forced him toward Ireland instead. A faint hope stirred in him that Ireland, which hated England, might give him help.

He was right. With England a common enemy, old scores were wiped out. The Earl of Cork urged him to remain. But within sight of home he regained his courage, sailing back to England in his one remaining ship, the *Destiny*.

On June 21, the *Destiny's* sails were sighted outside Plymouth Harbour. It was the twenty-second anniversary of the battle of Cadiz, where Raleigh had led the English fleet to victory.

Unfortunately the story of Raleigh's misfortunes had preceded him. He had hoped to bring it himself, and shape it a little in his service. But at the news of the burning of San Thomé Gondomar, the Spanish ambassador, had burst into the King's presence, shouting, Pirates! Pirates!" He demanded that James promise to deliver Raleigh to the Spanish for public hanging.

James agreed to this, but he said that Raleigh, as an Englishman, must have an official inquiry or else it would look too bad.

The people of London already dislike Gondomar. Shortly after Raleigh's return, a mob of several thousand roared their way into the Spanish embassy gardens, seeking a diplomat who had injured a child in the street. They began to shout in praise of Raleigh. Other crowds shouted for Raleigh. He became a symbol of the anti-Spanish feeling in Britain.

James wavered.

Gondomar then ordered the Privy Council — the governing body of England — to come to the Spanish embassy for his instructions. Such a demand was an outrage without precedent to British sovereignty.

Bess Raleigh meanwhile had ridden down to Plymouth to meet her husband. She was followed by Raleigh's cousin, Sir Lewis Stukeley, Vice-Admiral of Devon. Stukeley laughed and quipped with Raleigh, and at length told him lightly that he had been ordered to arrest him. There was no hurry, however; Raleigh could tend to any business he had. Stukeley himself would undertake the sale of the *Destiny's* cargo, the tobacco seized in Guiana.

E

Bess implored Raleigh to escape to France. She distrusted Stukeley — and all the world. She told her husband that Winwood, his only powerful friend in the government, had died while he was away, and she described the demonstration for Raleigh in London. She said that many wondered "extremely that so great a wise man as Sir Walter Raleigh should have returned to cast himself upon so inevitable a rock."

A French envoy also begged him to escape to France while there was time. The old offer stood: he could become an admiral in the French fleet.

It was even suggested that the King wanted him to escape and be spared a great embarrassment.

Raleigh refused. He said he would trust in the honour of his country. What did he mean? His country had showed no honour toward him.

He said that to escape would mean guilt. He was not guilty.

Bess was in despair. He tried to comfort her but he was very tired and his spirit cracked. If death waited for him at the hands of his countrymen, then toward death he would go. Bess wept and pleaded. He loved her, and at length he weakened.

A friend negotiated with the captain of a French ship, and that same night, before Raleigh could change his mind, rowed him out to the ship. But Raleigh *could* change his mind. As he was about to climb aboard, he drew back and said he would not disgrace himself. He must face what came and face it fighting.

He would not listen to Bess's pleas. Strict orders had now come to Stukeley to arrest Raleigh and bring him to London. They started immediately, and Raleigh came out of his odd daze.

If he did not prepare his defence before he reached London he would have no chance. He gambled for time and begged a French physician who was travelling in the group to help him simulate an illness. The doctor agreed.

Raleigh staggered, knocking his head against a pillar. Then he frightened everyone, except the doctor and Bess, by thrashing about on the floor, naked and in convulsions. When Stukeley rushed in and saw him in this state, he called for English doctors. In the interval the French physician rubbed an ointment into Raleigh's skin. It caused purple spots to break out on his face and chest. The English doctors drew back in alarm, and said to move him would be very dangerous.

Raleigh had never done such a wild, deceptive thing before. In the daytime he carried on the deception, eating nothing, groaning, waiting for the skin inflammation to subside. At night he ate ravenously the food smuggled to him, and wrote, at white heat, his famous *Apology for the Voyage to Guiana*. It was a brilliant defence. But in the act of writing it, he saw he had been a fool not to escape.

He sent Bess ahead to London to arrange with one of his friends to have a ketch ready in the Thames by which he could reach a French ship.

His cousin, Stukeley, meantime, was working his own unpleasant surprises. He was clinging to Raleigh like a shadow, and Raleigh with his odd careless trust answered all Stukeley's questions and so gave out his plans.

Stukeley offered to escape with him.

In the dark of the night they met Raleigh's friend, who had arranged for a wherry to row Raleigh to the ketch. They had not gone twenty strokes before Raleigh realised that another boat was following.

Stukeley soothed him. They continued to row down the river for an hour. Then, when no ketch could be found in the darkness, Raleigh knew he had been betrayed. At that moment, the other boat hailed them in the name of the King.

Still Stukeley reassured him and accepted certain valuables for Bess in case Raleigh moved into danger. It was not until the two boats had landed that Stukeley

showed his real colours. He arrested Raleigh and Raleigh's friend in the name of the King.

For a moment Raleigh was silent. Then he said quietly, "Sir Lewis, these actions will not turn out to your credit."

Stukeley laughed. He delivered Raleigh to the Tower and filched odds and ends from Raleigh's pockets; he also kept all the proceeds from the sale of the tobacco. He was in a merry mood.

When someone called him Sir Judas, he shrugged it off. When crowds called him Sir Judas, he became alarmed. When he returned to Devon to confer with the

old Lord Admiral, and heard even the Lord Admiral cry,
"What, thou base fellow! *Thou* — the scorn and contempt
of men, how darest thou offer thyself in my presence!"
Stukeley fled.

He complained to the King. James answered, "What
would you have me do? If I should hang all that speak
ill of thee, all the trees in my kingdom would not
suffice." Then the King fell to muttering, "I have done
amiss. Raleigh's blood be upon thy head."

Stukeley fled from England. Within two years he died
a raving lunatic.

16

A Brave Man Dies

Raleigh did not mind dying, but he minded very much being put to death unjustly. He wrote to Queen Anne begging her help.

She was now a sick woman and half out of her mind, but she had never faltered in her admiration for this man who had been her son's friend. She had no influence whatever with her husband, but she wrote a sad little note to the man she knew could sway the King. This was his current favourite — the Duke of Buckingham. She begged that "Sir Walter Raleigh's life may not be called in question . . ."

But Buckingham had decided that the marriage of the King's son Charles to a Spanish princess was as important to him as to the King, and he knew that Raleigh's life was a part of the price being asked.

The only question that remained was how to offer this sacrifice of The Old Pirate. What reason could be given for hanging him? By common law, a man indicted for treason could not be charged with a new crime. Many believed that this protected Raleigh. A commission was appointed to "investigate." Bacon, who had assured Raleigh before he left that no pardon was needed, headed the commission. Coke was a member.

For two months they examined witnesses. They questioned Raleigh's seamen; they questioned French agents about Raleigh's plans to seek refuge in France.

Gondomar notified James that the King of Spain wished Raleigh hanged in England, not in Spain. Philip III had written his ambassador, "exaggerate as much as you can Raleigh's guilt and try to get the King to make a great demonstration . . . Make him understand that I am offended and that if a proper remedy be not forthcoming at once, we shall make reprisals and seize English property in Spain." He did not add (because he did not need to) that the marriage arrangements between James's son and his daughter were at a delicate state. This marriage was the basis of James's foreign policy.

Ironically, it was Coke's conscience that caused delays. Coke had come to fear and distrust Spain almost as much as Raleigh. He thought that to hand over to the Spaniards an English subject, a man who had distinguished himself in the fight against Spain, was an abomination.

Coke wrote to James and urged a public trial where Raleigh could be heard in his own defence before the entire Privy Council and certain judges. He urged even more that the chamber be opened to any nobleman or gentleman who might care to appear as a witness.

Once Raleigh's request for only one witness had been refused. Now his old enemy was suggesting dozens in his behalf. Let this be *English* justice, Coke argued, and let all the world see how fair it is.

James did not like Coke's advice in any way. It would be impossible to appease Gondomar with such an action. He reminded Coke that at his trial in 1603 Raleigh had "by his wit turned the hatred of men into compassion."

Hour by hour, Raleigh was asked questions to trap him. He defended himself skilfully. That is to say, he spoke only the truth, but the truth was not what would save him. All that the state really wanted was a decent reason to offer him up to the executioner. This he steadily refused to provide. He seemed almost to enjoy muddling his questioners.

But he was sick. His heart was desperately heavy. Bess also was imprisoned, and they wrote constantly to each other. "My love I send you that you may keep it when I am dead . . . I would not with my last will present you with sorrows, dear Bess. Let them go to the grave with me and be buried in the dust. Bear my destruction gently, and with a heart like yourself."

Though he prepared for death, he clung to one hope: the fact that Guiana had never been Spanish, and the King himself had confirmed England's claims.

But Bacon, speaking for the commissioners, laboured long over Raleigh's attack on Spanish lives and property in Guiana and his "abuse of the King's confidence." He said that Raleigh must die because he had been sentenced to death fifteen years before. Bacon was the very man who had assured Raleigh that a pardon was not necessary.

The tragic farce came to an end. Once more legal flummery was carried through. The King's Bench must authorise the execution of his 1603 sentence.

Raleigh was roused early in the morning of October 28 to come before the justices. He was feverish and shaking with ague; his hair was now perfectly white. He had to walk in procession from the Tower to Westminster — the width of the entire city of London.

As he stood before the court, the new Attorney General, Sir Henry Yelverton, seemed for a moment to catch a glimpse of greatness. Although he called for the execution, he said, "Sir Walter Raleigh hath been a statesman and a man who, in respect of his parts and quality, is to be pitied. He hath been as a star at which the world gazed. But stars must fall whey they trouble the sphere wherein they abide."

James signed the death warrant that day and insisted that the execution take place the next morning. He listened to no one. Many pleaded with him — the Queen, members of the Privy Council, the Bishop of Winchester, and Raleigh's son Carew, now thirteen years old. And, remarkably enough, even a Spanish priest, lately come to London, said that Raleigh's death would injure English relations with Spain "if he were sacrificed to the malice of the Spaniards."

But James was sick and tired of the name of Raleigh. He insisted stubbornly that the execution must take place on the Lord Mayor's Day, for all the processions and excitement would keep the crowds away from the execution of "one of the gallantest worthies that ever England bred."

Poor James. . . . One more miscalculation. When Raleigh was brought out to die, the courtyard could not contain the crowds come to do him honour. They overflowed the streets in all directions, and the Lord Mayor's Show was forgotten.

Bess had been with her husband the night before. She could hardly believe that the end of all their dreams had come. She had clung to him in a frenzy. "God hold me in my wits — how can I bear it!"

Raleigh had comforted her in every way he could, but he probably knew that her greatest comfort would be the marriage they had shared. The Council had promised her Raleigh's body for burial — a favour which was not always granted. Raleigh made a little joke of it as he held her in his arms.

"It is well, dear Bess, that thou mayest dispose of that dead which thou hadst not always the disposing of when alive."

As dawn came, he had written a poem in the flyleaf of his Bible.

> *Even such is Time! who takes in trust*
> *Our Youth, our joys and all we have,*
> *And pays us but with earth and dust;*
> *Who in the dark and silent grave,*
> *When we have wandered all our ways*
> *Shuts up the story of our days.*
> *But from that earth, that grave, that dust,*
> *The Lord shall raise me up, I trust.*

He seemed positively light-hearted. The attending minister reproached him for not thinking on death. Raleigh said, "What is death but an opinion and imagination? Though to others (my way) might seem grievous, yet I had rather die so than of a burning fever."

He insisted on a good breakfast and a pipe of tobacco. Then he dressed himself with great care.

It was a bitter cold morning, and Raleigh's only fear was that the cold would accentuate his ague and make the people think he was quaking from fear.

All his friends were there, some on horses around the scaffold, others in windows overlooking the Yard. They wished to show their support and send him on his way with their gestures of affection.

He talked to the crowd, explaining that he was in no way afraid to die. He said he was sorry that his voice was weak for he would like to be heard by his friends in the windows.

The Earl of Arundel called out, "We will come down to you." Pushing their way through the crowd, the Earl and several lords climbed to the scaffold, shook his hand, and stood there listening carefully as he spoke. He offered his full defence again, and it was a profoundly moving speech because he sought above everything to clear his name for the sake of his wife and son.

When he finished, he asked them all to join him in a prayer, and then he spread out his hands.

"I have a long journey," he said, "and must now bid the company farewell."

He took off his ruff and his doublet, and asked to see the axe. When the headsman hesitated, he said, "I prithee, let me see it. Dost thou think I am afraid of it?" Smiling he spoke to the sheriff. "This is sharp medicine, but it is a sure cure for all diseases."

His courage moved everyone. The Spanish agent who witnessed it reported to Madrid, "Raleigh's spirit never faltered, nor did his countenance change."

He asked the headsman to take his command from

him. "When I stretch forth my hands, dispatch me." He knelt and put his head on the block and spread out his hands. But the headsman could not lift his arms.

"What dost thou fear?" Raleigh asked him. "Strike, man, strike!"

The axe fell. The executioner held up the head, still beautiful as when he had been a young man. A long sigh went over the crowd.

Someone called out, "We have not another such head to be cut off."

James found it necessary to put out a long statement on the reasons for the execution. Raleigh had brought back no gold; he had broken the peace with Spain.

But Raleigh's death strengthened the Protestant, anti-Spanish feeling as he, alive, had never done.

Prince Charles married a French princess.

Gondomar dared not venture on to the streets in his litter. "There goes the devil in a dungcart!" people cried after him.

When James died, and later when his son Charles was executed, Raleigh's name was invoked again and again.

His greenest memory lies in a most subtle way in America which he loved. He envisioned America as a community of men, women, and children having incentive, in a broad free world, to make homes and to prosper.

BIBLIOGRAPHY

Akrigg, George P. V.: *Jacobean Pageant; Or, The Court of King James I.* Hamish Hamilton, 1962.

Bowen, Catherine D.: *The Lion and the Throne: The Life and Times of Sir Edward Coke.* Hamish Hamilton, 1957.

Bullett, Gerald W. (Editor): *Silver Poets of the Sixteenth Century.* J. M. Dent, 1960. Paperback edition: J. M. Dent.

Irwin, Margaret: *That Great Lucifer; A Portrait of Sir Walter Raleigh.* Chatto & Windus, 1960. Paperback edition: Penguin Books.

Jenkins, Elizabeth: *Elizabeth the Great.* Victor Gollancz, 1956.

McElwee, William: *The Wisest Fool in Christendom.* Faber & Faber, 1958.

Mattingly, Garrett: *The Defeat of the Spanish Armada.* Jonathan Cape, 1959. Paperback edition: Penguin Books.

Neale, John E.: *Queen Elizabeth.* Jonathan Cape, 1934. Paperback edition: Penguin Books.

Nicoll, Allardyce (Editor): *The Elizabethans.* Cambridge University Press, 1957.

Oakeshott, Walter F.: *The Queen and the Poet.* Faber & Faber, 1960. A Study of Elizabeth and Raleigh.

Rowse, A. L.: *Raleigh and the Throckmortons.* Macmillan, 1962.

Tillyard, E. M. W.: *The Elizabethan World Picture.* Chatto & Windus, 1943. Paperback edition: Penguin Books.

Waldman, Milton: *Sir Walter Raleigh.* William Collins, 1943.

Index